FOUR YEARS IN A RED HELL

The Story of Father Rigney

FOUR YEARS
IN A RED HELL

The Story of FATHER RIGNEY

by HAROLD W. RIGNEY, S.V.D.

Divine Word Missionary

HENRY REGNERY COMPANY 1956
Chicago

DEDICATION

To my dear stepmother, Mrs. Addie Rigney, my dear brother and sisters, Reverend Doctor J. Francis Rigney, Mrs. Mildred Derby, Mrs. Mary Anne Hanley, Mrs. Dorothy Haggerty, Mrs. Helen Brady, and their families, and all, especially the Divine Word Missionaries (S.V.D.), Msgr. Thomas A. Meehan, the clergy, sisters, and all the Catholic laity, young and old, of Chicagoland, Joseph B. Meegan, Thomas F. Reynolds, and members of the Senate and Lower House of the U. S. Congress and the U. S. State Department, who by prayer and petition obtained my release from prison, to the noble German and Chinese Holy Ghost Missionary Sisters (S.Sp.S.), my last friends in Peking, who stood by me and helped me in days that were bitter, and to the persecuted Catholics of China and their heroic martyrs and confessors.

PREFACE

ON FEBRUARY 1, 1949, Peiping (Peking), China was captured by the communists.

From then until July 25, 1951, I daily expected to be arrested by the communists in reprisal for my fight before and after their capture of Peiping, to preserve the Fu Jen Catholic University of Peking (Peiping), over which I was rector, as a true center of culture.

On July 25, 1951, I was arrested by the Chinese communist Sepo (Security Police, the Gestapo of Red China), on unjust, false and outrageous grounds. After a veritable hell of four years and two months of physical and mental tortures, I was released from prison on September 11, 1955, as a result of the prayers and written petitions of my relatives and many friends in the U.S.A. and other parts of the world.

I was then expelled from communist China into the free territory of Her Majesty's Crown Colony of Hong Kong, on September 16, 1955.

In the following pages, I have attempted to describe the experience of my imprisonment of 50 months in the city that is now called Peking, China.

I wish to thank the Reverend Henry Striethorst, S.V.D., Superior of the Divine Word Mission, 10 Tung Shan Terrace, Stubbs Road, Hong Kong, and his secretary, Mrs. Elizabeth Lee Solabarrieta, as well as the Very Reverend Lawrence G. Mack, S.V.D. Provincial, and the Reverend Ralph M. Wiltgen, S.V.D., both of St. Mary Mission Seminary, Techny, Illinois, U.S.A., for their help in the preparation of the manuscript.

HAROLD W. RIGNEY, S.V.D., *Rector,*
THE FU JEN CATHOLIC UNIVERSITY OF PEKING,
PEKING (PEIPING), CHINA.

CONTENTS

CONTENTS—continued

The Struggle to Safeguard Fu Jen
Catholic University

"YOU ARE ARRESTED as an American spy," said a woman member of the Sepo (Security Police) who had accompanied the police to my living quarters where they had hand-cuffed me. As she spoke, she held up to my view a small piece of paper with Chinese characters on it.

I was arrested!

I was arrested as a spy—an American spy!

For five years I had fought the Chinese communists, in my efforts to protect the Fu Jen Catholic University of Peking from their poisonous infiltrations and their disturbing, destructive tactics. In the latter part of this period, I had tried to preserve this university, as a citadel of learning and true culture, from being taken over by the communist government.

These were my "crimes," the real reasons for my arrest.

However, I was not charged with doing all this but with being a spy.

The communists had forcibly taken over the Fu Jen Catholic University of Peking on 12 October, 1950, where I was the rector. They wanted to justify this theft by libeling this university as a center of American espionage. They began by libeling me, the rector, as an American spy.

I thought of how Christ was charged with being a counter-revolutionary, a spy, to use the jargon of present day com-

---

NOTE. In this book the names of prisoners, aside from myself, are fictitious.

1

munists, and not with being the Messiah. I thought of how Nero in his attempt to destroy Christianity burned Christians alive under charges of being saboteurs, counter-revolutionaries or spies who set Rome ablaze, and not for being Christians. So on down the ages, the persecutors of the followers of Christ, the Neros of the past, as well as those of the present: Lenin, Stalin, Hitler, Tito, Mao Tse-tung, have followed the same tactics of accusing, imprisoning and killing the followers of Christ under the title of counter-revolutionaries, saboteurs, spies and what not, for anything but being the Christians they hate, whose religion they seek to destroy.

I felt I had noble forerunners and my handcuffs were no disgrace but an honor.

The "People's" government of China may call me a spy, but I am not and never was a spy.

I often thought that according to the Chinese communists, every one who enjoys the faculties of sense perception, as seeing, hearing, smelling, is apt to be accused of collecting intelligence: of being a spy. Reading the local Chinese communist newspaper, looking out the window and noting that it rained, hearing the price of food on the market, have all been declared by the communist courts of China as collecting intelligence.

Moreover, anyone exercising their faculties of communicating, as speaking, writing, is apt to be accused of reporting intelligence: of being a spy. Writing about news items of the local communist press, writing a letter in which one states that it rained, telling another the price of shao mi (millet), have been declared by these same communist courts as reporting intelligence.

It was in mid December 1946, that I learned of the general strike at Fu Jen. I was in Shanghai, where I had gone to welcome His Excellency Archbishop Antonio Riberi, the newly arrived Internuncio to China.

There had been agitation instigated among the students of Fu Jen by an evidently organized student group of subversive agents. This culminated in a general strike, in December, 1946, over an increase in dormitory fees to meet with the increase in the inflation of the Chinese currency. Any fair minded person acquainted with the conditions of China at that time would have made no objections to this increase which was normal.

From my investigations I concluded that this subversive group were communists. I was shocked to think that a handful of communists could exercise such influence in the Fu Jen Catholic University where the Catholic students were certainly as numerous if not more numerous than the communists, although about 90% of our students were non-Catholics, mostly pagans with a few Protestants and Mohammedans.

Did the Catholic students appreciate what was done for them at Fu Jen? Were they slumbering, inert, overcome by a feeling of false security, instead of being alert, aroused and active to protect their university and fight for their rights to study in peace? These thoughts plagued me on my return to Peiping when negotiations were carried on to settle the strike and allow over 2,500 university students to pursue the ends for which they had come to Fu Jen: to study, to be allowed the peace and quiet needed to cultivate their minds by studying, instead of agitations aroused by agents of a Stalin-Mao Tze-tung conspiracy little concerned with the true welfare of these very students and their fatherland, China.

The Catholic students of Fu Jen did appreciate what was being done for them at Fu Jen, as I soon learned. They were not inert, they were ready to fight for their university and their right to study in peace. They only needed leadership. This was supplied them by courageous Chinese priests, who were also students at Fu Jen. Once these brave students were organized, I gave them advice and directions in the struggle. As a consequence, we defeated every attempt of the commu-

3

nists to lead the Fu Jen students into strikes and street demonstrations during 1947. We helped the students to avoid participating in such as the strike and demonstration planned for January 1947, under the cloak of an anti-civil war movement, and another, an anti-American strike and demonstration scheduled for the beginning of June 1947. These were so many "crimes" of mine: sabotaging the "progressive" movement at Fu Jen.

This brief account does not permit a full and complete statement of the various tricks and attacks the communists instigated at Fu Jen as well as the fight we made against them. While other universities of Peiping area were disturbed by strikes and other forms of communist subversive activities, Fu Jen enjoyed relative peace.

I think back to those days, with great admiration for those Catholic students and their brave fighting spirit.

God bless them!

·2·

More "Crimes"

DURING THE SECOND WORLD WAR, Fu Jen continued to carry on under the leadership of German Divine Word Missionaries, or members of the Society of the Divine Word (in Latin, Societas Verbi Divini—S.V.D.), who strove to preserve the university as a center of true culture, for the Church. They put up a good fight but since the university was in that part of China controlled by the Japanese, they were obliged to observe the regulations of the local Japanese government. However, and this is important, they continued to be recognized by the National Government of China, in Chungking. The Japanese tried to take over all of Fu Jen. They did take over the Fu Jen's Boys' Middle School and then tried to take over Fu Jen University. The Very Reverend Rudolf Rahmann, S.V.D., rector of Fu Jen, fought to regain the middle school and he succeeded. He also successfully fought and saved the university. For all this, he deserves much credit.

When however the fighting of the second World War was over, there was fear that the Nationalist Government would confiscate Fu Jen as German property as they did the German hospital at Peiping, Divine Word mission property as in Ishui-Wan Chuang, diocese of Ichoufu, Shantung, and the properties of private Germans.

There was evidence that a group of staff members of Fu Jen planned with the help of the Nanking government to oust the Divine Word Missionaries as Germans and take over and control Fu Jen. It so happens that I knew quite a lot about this. How later these same staff members, full of smiles, with-

5

out a wrinkle of shame, could meet me, is something I could never fathom. At any rate, I considered they were anything but pleased with me for helping to thwart their plans and their smiles were not to express joy and friendliness at seeing me but to cover feelings that were quite the contrary.

The rector, Father Rahmann, still fighting to preserve Fu Jen, declared that Fu Jen was American property and he was correct.

Fu Jen had been founded by American Benedictines who bought the property which they registered as American property, and developed Fu Jen University according to American pattern. When the Divine Word Missionaries and especially the American province of this society succeeded the American Benedictines as the administrators of Fu Jen, they perpetuated Fu Jen as an American-owned, American patterned institution. There were Divine Word Missionaries of American nationalities as well as other nationalities, especially Germans, on the faculties. During the second World War, when the American Divine Word Missionaries were placed in concentration camps, the German confreres continued, with increasing numbers, to represent the Divine Word Missionaries at Fu Jen, without essentially changing the American character of Fu Jen.

It was quite easy for an opportunistic group, after the Pacific War, to point to Fu Jen as a German institution and the Divine Word Missionaries there as agents of the German and Japanese governments. These missionaries, under great difficulties, had only carried on a project of the Church and were able to do so because of their nationality. I have great respect for these fathers. Their chief concern was to hold, to save an institution of the Church. Hence, when Japanese influence in China was replaced by American influence, they yielded with no resentment or ill will that I ever detected, and stepped to one side to allow American Divine Word Missionaries to occupy the key positions.

It was in these circumstances that I, as an American, was sent to Fu Jen. I had been on the teaching staff and served as Catholic chaplain at Achimota College—now the University College, Gold Coast, British West Africa. In November 1942, I was commissioned in Accra (Gold Coast capital) in the U. S. Army, as a chaplain assigned to the U. S. Army Air Force and served in that capacity until February 1946. In May 1946, I was sent to Peiping to the Divine Word community of Fu Jen. In July, 1946, I was appointed rector of Fu Jen University and rector of the Divine Word community there. On August 4th, 1946, I took over these two offices.

I was given these appointments not because of great scholarship, which I do not have, or a rich background of experience in China, which I did not have, but because I was an American, an ex-commissioned officer and chaplain, fresh from the U. S. Army, with a Doctor of Philosophy degree in Geology.

Since Fu Jen had been known as an American institution, the American Consul General in Peiping gave Rector Rahmann to understand that it would be more fitting to have an American as rector of Fu Jen.

I eventually became this American rector.

Hence, the communists accused me of being sent to take over German influence. This was a great "crime." The only German influence, if one could call it such, which I took over, was a community of some forty Divine Word priests and brothers, which was 90% German.

When I arrived in Peiping in June 1946, there were American servicemen there of the Army and Marines. I met many of these and as an ex-army chaplain, enjoyed their company. Among these servicemen I met, were personnel of O.S.S. (Office of Strategic Service).

The Peiping O.S.S. approached me on one occasion asking me if I knew whether a radio of the former German Embassy, which had been used for monitoring messages, was hidden in Fu Jen. I felt the honor of the university was at stake and made an investigation of the university buildings and grounds without discovering any evidence of such a radio. I told this officer that I could find no radio as he had described. Later, the communists learned of this from a Chinese prisoner, at Ts'ao Lan Tzu prison, who had worked for O.S.S. with, I am told, the rank of a colonel. They accused me of serving as an O.S.S., since I had conducted an investigation for them. They totally disregarded the fact that I simply investigated the university over which I was rector.

I also told an O.S.S. officer rumors of the countryside to the effect that the communist troops near Peiping had been seen with American side arms and an American ambulance that had disappeared from American control, and that Soviet technicians had been seen with the Chinese communist army in Jehol. This was all considered as military intelligence by the communists.

Another activity that aroused the ire of the communists was a survey of the Catholic Church of North China as of June, 1947. This survey was conducted to learn the true nature of the Church in North China as affected by the communists and inform my ecclesiastical and religious superiors. The latter were responsible to the Congregation of the Propagation of the Faith in Rome, for the administration of Fu Jen University, an important Church institution in North China. The survey was also intended to acquaint the general public through the press about the condition of the Church in communist occupied areas.

In December 1946, there were many missionaries: bishops, priests, sisters, and brothers, Chinese and foreign, in Peiping from outside dioceses or missions. Most of them had been expelled from their missions by the communists.

I organized a committee, representative of leading mission

bodies and various nationalities of North China, who had members then in Peiping: a German Divine Word Missionary; a French Jesuit; a Belgian Scheut; a Dutch Franciscan; a Chinese Lazarist and myself, an American Divine Word Missionary. This committee collected data, mostly from bishops and superiors then in Peiping, which was assembled and published in a final report. It dealt with the personnel, Chinese and foreign; physical plants as churches, schools, rectories, convents, hospitals, orphanages; as well as religious activities of the Church, and all this before and after the occupation of the communists. Some thirty-five dioceses or about 50% of North China were covered which gave a good cross section of North China. A missionary who had gone through the siege and fall of Yenchowfu, Shantung, described his experience. Another missionary described the capture by the communists of Si Wan Tze or Chung Li in Charhar. These two descriptions were incorporated into the report.

This report was sent to H. E. Archbishop Riberi, Internuncio; to my superiors in Rome and Father Ralph, S.V.D., in Chicago. Copies were shown to a friend of mine in O.S.S. and to a colonel in the American Section of the Executive Headquarters of Peiping who had given me an outline map of the parts of China occupied by communists, such as would appear in newspapers. I also showed the report to two journalists who wrote articles based on it for a big New York paper and for the American Catholic Press. This survey was called a great "crime" by the communists, a big "spying program" that collected and disseminated social, religious, economic and military intelligence.

From August 1946, when I became rector, to January 1951, when I was succeeded by Father Peter Sun, S.V.D., as rector of the Fu Jen Divine Word Community, I sent monthly reports to my Superior General in Rome, who was also Chancellor of Fu Jen. In these reports I acquainted the Chancellor

9

with the events at Fu Jen as well as local conditions affecting the university and the expenses of conducting it. A copy of this report was sent to Father Ralph, S.V.D., who raised most of the funds needed to maintain Fu Jen.* He had requested me to keep him informed of affairs at Fu Jen to help him in his journalistic and publicity activities for the university. I also kept Archbishop Riberi, the Internuncio, informed of affairs at Fu Jen. All this according to the communists was "criminal": collecting and submitting intelligence to the Vatican and to the U. S. Government.

In the spring and summer of 1948, when the victorious communist armies in the Northeast (Manchuria) captured Mukden and swept down past the great wall, there was much alarm at Fu Jen and other universities.

Many students and staff members fled to the South to avoid the expected harshness and cruelties of the communists.

Others advocated moving Fu Jen to the South or to Taiwan (Formosa) which I did not favor since I believed that if Peiping fell, the South and Taiwan would eventually fall.

On putting the matter up to His Excellency, Archbishop Riberi, Internuncio, in October 1948, I was instructed by His Excellency not to move but to remain. In the event of Peiping falling to the communists, I should, he said, try to work out a modus vivendi or reasonable working agreement with them that would allow the university to carry on.

In the autumn of 1948, some of the leading staff members of Fu Jen advised and urged us foreign fathers and sisters to leave Fu Jen and Peiping to save ourselves from being killed by the communists when they came. I had reason to believe that this advice was prompted mostly by a desire to induce us Divine Word Missionaries to leave so that the lay staff

---

* Rev. Father Ralph, S.V.D., is National Director of "S.V.D. Catholic Universities," 316 N. Michigan, Chicago, Illinois.

which was mostly non-Catholic could take over the university and then offer it to the communists in atonement for their past Kuomintang activities. I replied that fathers and sisters who could be declared surplus would leave but a few of us would remain to negotiate a working agreement with the communists. At any rate, we would remain at the university as long as we could, and hold on to as much as we could.

Later in October and November 1948, this same group organized a staff union. To me, this looked very much like another attempt to organize the staff to be prepared to take over the university when the communists came, and offer it to them. I counteracted by inducing all the fathers and sisters to join the new staff union and with the help of their votes elect a body of officers who would cooperate with us to negotiate a working agreement with the communists and save the university for the Church. After this election, the movement died out. No more meetings were held. For this, the communists accused me of sabotaging the "progressive" movement at Fu Jen.

In mid-December, the communist armies closed in on Peiping, surrounding and laying siege to the city.

On February 1, 1949, their armies led by Lin Piao entered Peiping after the nationalist general, Fu Tso-I had surrendered with his rich military supplies and large armies. He was later rewarded with the post of Minister of Water Conservancy of the communist government of the "People's Republic" of China.

Peiping soon became the capital of Communist China and was renamed Peking.

Still More "Crimes"

WE WERE THEN in communist controlled territory. Our plight at Fu Jen entered another phase.

Some staff members wrote strong, offensive articles accusing us Divine Word Missionaries, especially me, of being imperialists. These were published in the local newspapers, now under communist control.

I soon embarked on a policy of coming to a working agreement with the new order, as Archbishop Riberi had instructed me.

I offered to remove some foreign fathers and sisters from key positions and indicated a desire to enter into conference with competent government officials and representatives of the various groups of the university to work out a modus vivendi.

There was good will and sincerity on the part of the Divine Word Missionaries but the "progressive" leaders of the Fu Jen staff under the control of the communists showed no such willingness. They replied by heaping more abuse on us Divine Word Missionaries, especially foreign members. They completely ignored us and formed a committee to reorganize the university. I sought representation for the Church on this committee since Fu Jen was an institution of the Church but my many proposals in this regard were completely ignored or rejected.

The university was to be reorganized without representation on the part of the Church, without considering the wishes or suggestions of the Church which had founded, built and financed Fu Jen since 1925.

This effort of mine to obtain representation of the Church on the university reformation committee, was later held against me as a "crime" of opposing and sabotaging the revolution. Again, this made me a "counter-revolutionary."

In the spring of 1949, in the midst of the fight to save Fu Jen, I was warned that a group of "progressives" planned to capture me. This was to be done after dark when I returned on my bicycle to the university. The "progressives" were to take me to some hide-out, beat me up and torture me until I promised to give them the gold the Divine Word Society had to finance the university until June 30, 1949, the end of the fiscal year.

I could take no chances with this report. It probably was false as there were reasons that militated against it. It was also probably true, as there were reasons that supported it.

So to protect myself, when I left the university alone on my bicycle, I varied my routes from trip to trip and never returned over the same route I had taken from the university. If a gang of "progressives" wanted to waylay me, the probability of avoiding them was in my favor.

Being followed was another probability I had to cope with. Often when cycling through Peking I would make a detour into a net of hutungs or lanes, making several sharp turns to elude a possible tracer.

Another ruse of mine, on long open streets, was to ride fast for about half a mile then suddenly slow up, get off my bicycle and occupy myself with adjusting some part of the chain. A tracer would be obliged to continue at a rapid rate taking a lead far ahead of me. He could not slacken his rate, stop or turn around without giving himself away. After a few minutes, I would mount my bicycle and slowly ride, making a turn to further evade the possible tracer.

I resorted to another stratagem when the bicycle traffic was heavy by turning up a side hutung, riding a hundred or more feet, then stopping to dismount, examine a part of the bicycle, and slowly turn around and ride back, continuing on the first busy street. The tracer, if he observed me make the turn into the hutung, would be obliged to follow me up the hutung and ride far past me, only to lose me when I rode away in the opposite direction.

In the land of the police state of the red star, the system of spying on people, keeping track of their movements, occupations, activities, contacts, statements, etc., is organized as never before. I often thought that Red China might have a chance to succeed if the manpower and hours of labor devoted to police work, to witch hunting, to spying on every single person in the land, were devoted to real production of food or other material wealth.

However, this is impossible in a communist country because communism is so contrary to human desires and aspirations that it can maintain itself only by force, by the police state.

This misuse of labor increases with the years because the witch hunters continually pursue their searchings. As time goes on, the mass of dossiers accumulates and more and more witch hunters are needed to guard these bigger and bigger mountains of dossiers as well as to continually go through them, studying them and preparing new arrests. Arrests, imprisonments, sentences and executions do not reduce or keep this mass of material down, since the dossiers of such victims are kept and restudied for more arrests.

A European member of the Fu Jen staff told me that my waste paper basket was checked each night after I had left my office. I decided to give witch hunters and their running dogs on the university maintenance staff a little extra and fruitless work. I often tore a letter in halves. One half I burned and the other I tore into tiny pieces smaller than postage stamps which I mixed up and threw in my waste paper basket. Some witch hunter spent hours of labor piecing these together only to discover he had half a letter.

Often I received a letter from the British Council Library inviting me to some exhibition or lecture at their library. These letters with their large British Council letter heads were sometimes torn up by me to small bits and thrown in the waste basket to give the witch hunters a little exercise. The letter head must have aroused their interest in piecing together a letter that turned out to be only an invitation.

Such activities of eluding and teasing the witch hunters of chairman Mao Tse-tung must have brought punishment on me. The communists could not mention these by way of accusations or "crimes." Such would have spelled loss of face for them. But they could, and I am sure they did, wreak their vengeance on me under cover of false accusations of spying or the like.

Often, later in prison, I felt that the communists had a special hatred of me for the loss of face they suffered when I thwarted and exposed their dirty tactics. To mention one or the other instance: I prevented many of their strikes and demonstrations at Fu Jen. I offered to talk matters over concerning Fu Jen, as they tell the world they like to do, but they refused to negotiate for fear of losing some ground. I thwarted their plans to induce the Fu Jen Catholics to petition them to take over Fu Jen. I maneuvered the Fu Jen case to the point where poor little Minister of Education Ma, with a communist at his side whispering instructions to him, stated to me in a conference that the only connection the Church could have with Fu Jen was to finance it. The Church financing Fu Jen, a communist controlled center of anti-religious, communist activities!

The communists lost much face in their struggle in and over

Fu Jen and I was responsible for much of it. Therefore they hated me, calumniated me and punished me.

It was evident that my phone was tapped. Whenever I received a call from a party outside the university and I began to speak, the connections were often cut off for a few seconds then remade. This seemed like time out to make connections with a recording machine.

My suspicions were confirmed in the latter part of September, 1950.

Father William Hogan, S.V.D., the last of the American fathers to leave Fu Jen and Peking before me, had departed to Tientsin enroute to Taku Bar for a ship back to the "old country."

In Tientsin he phoned me, asking me to send him the twenty-one copies of the list of the contents of his trunks, which he had left behind since the highly "efficient" communist authorities for some unearthly reasons needed these twenty-one duplicates.

I told him that I would get them and send them to him immediately. I then left my office to search Father Hogan's former living quarters for them.

On returning to my office, my secretary, an elderly lady, told me she had just started to phone and to her utter amazement heard a conversation between Father Hogan and me. She was perplexed and told me what she had heard. It was the end of my recent conversation with Father Hogan.

After a moment's consideration, I told her there was nothing strange or mysterious about this. It was just another blunder of the communist police and a proof that they were tapping my phone. These witch hunters, I explained to her, had made a mistake of sending out the end of my conversation of the last call instead of recording the new phone call.

When a new university senate was to be formed at Fu Jen, in June 1949, I requested and finally obtained two of the nineteen seats on it for the Church. This was also a "crime" of mine—a plot to sabotage the reformation of Fu Jen.

After all my efforts to negotiate a modus vivendi had failed, I followed a delaying policy, a rear guard action, playing for time, hoping against hope for a change either in the government or government policy. I held on to posts as long as possible. This was also a "crime": working against the government.

In the spring of 1950, I tried to prevent the issuing of new contracts to five members of the Fu Jen teaching staff, who had demonstrated open hostility to the Church and us Divine Word Missionaries in such a manner that it was impossible for us to continue on the staff. I later withdrew this request since it was contrary to the regulations of the Ministry of Education, as I was told. This request of mine was also a crime: against the "People" of China.

·4·

"Father, Forgive Them"

AROUND THE BEGINNING of October, 1950, when the Ministry of Education of the communist government of Peking was planning to take over Fu Jen, a Catholic member of the staff who had gone over to the communist side, becoming a "progressive" or "reformed" Catholic, wrote a petition requesting the communist government to take over Fu Jen.

He then called representatives of the Catholic students and Catholic members of the teaching, administrative and maintenance staff of Fu Jen, and instructed these representatives to secure the signatures of all the Fu Jen Catholics to this petition.

I learned of this and told the students they were free to sign or not to sign, but if they did sign, they would be separating themselves from the fathers.

As a result of this expressed opinion of mine, none of the students signed this disgraceful petition and they even prevailed on five of the seven staff members who had signed, to retract their signatures.

Consequently, when the communists took over the university, there was no petition presented, signed by all the Catholics of Fu Jen, requesting the theft of Fu Jen, as the communists had planned. This action of mine was another of my many "crimes" of sabotaging the revolution.

On October 12, when the formal taking over of Fu Jen occurred, I had the speeches of the occasion, including that of Ma, Minister of Education, taken down in shorthand, translated and sent to my Superior General in Rome, who was Chancellor of Fu Jen University, to Archbishop Riberi, Internuncio, and to Father Ralph, S.V.D., of Chicago, Illinois, U.S.A., who raised most of the funds to operate Fu Jen. This was also a "crime" of collecting and submitting intelligence to my superiors, accused of serving as agents of the Vatican, and to Father Ralph, accused of being an agent of the U. S. Government.

Around the end of 1949, a person whom I knew, who worked in the Municipal Foreign Office of Peking, told me that the staff of the office had discussed a plan to take over the former military barracks of the U. S. Consulate General in Peking, which had become the main buildings of the consulate. In a conversation I had with a friend in the American Consulate, I told him about this discussion. This was a multiple "crime" according to the communists: prying into government plans, bribing cadres and passing on intelligence to the U. S. government.

The same person in the municipal government also told me that the communist government had planned to take over all private schools, including universities, within two years. This was a double "crime" of mine, according to the communists: collecting intelligence and bribing cadres.

Around the time the Sino-Soviet Treaty of Friendship was published, two persons in Peking told me they had heard the main contents of the treaty regarding allowing the Soviets the use of Port Arthur and the joint development of mineral deposits by the Soviets and Chinese in the Northwest. I told this to a friend of mine in the U. S. consulate, a day or so before the treaty was published in Peking. This was a "crime" according to the communists: collecting intelligence and reporting it to the U. S. government.

In the summer of 1950, Prime Minister Chou En-lai had a conference with the Chinese leaders of various Protestant bodies in Peking. An account of this meeting was published in a Peking daily paper. I had this article translated, since the discussion it reported indicated the policy of the government towards all Christian Churches, including the Catholic Church. I sent copies of this translation to Archbishop Riberi, Internuncio to China, as well as to my Superior General in Rome. This was a "crime" according to the communists: collecting intelligence and reporting it to the Vatican.

Shortly after this, I made a statement to the Catholic students and staff of Fu Jen on the "Three Self Movement." The movement was so called after the triple slogan:

"Self-government, self-support, and self-propagation of the Church."

This slogan expressed the principles for the reformation of the Christian Churches, Protestant and Catholic, of China.

I told these Catholics of Fu Jen that we Catholics favoured the principles of self-support and self-propagation of the Catholic Church in China, and we had always worked for the realization of these.

The third principle, however, self government, was not clear. If it meant that the Catholic Church of China should have a Chinese clergy, that is, Chinese bishops and Chinese priests, united and subject to the Bishop of Rome, the Pope, then we could support this principle, but if it meant that the Church of China was to be independent of the Bishop of Rome, the Pope, then we did not and would not support it, and nothing, death itself, could shake us from this our stand of union with the Pope.

This union with the Bishop of Rome was essential to our Catholic faith and religion. To break it would destroy our faith. It would be apostasy.

I then added that since the "People's" Government of China guaranteed freedom of religion, there was no need for Catholics to separate from Rome. I exhorted my hearers to remain steadfast in their faith, come what may.

God bless those stout hearted Chinese Catholics.

Most of them have preserved their faith in the present persecution of the Church in China, a persecution seldom paralleled in history in cunning, in malice, in thoroughness and in ferocity!

I repeated this instruction and exhortation once or twice in public and often in private conversations with Catholics.

All this was "criminal" according to the communists: "crimes" against the "people" of China, "crimes" of sabotage of the religious reformation movement in the New China.

In the end of September I had a meeting with Minister of Education Ma, who told me that the only connection the Church could continue to have with Fu Jen would be the financing of the university. The Church could not exercise any administrative control over Fu Jen. I then asked if this control included the forming of the Board of Trustees. To this he replied, "Yes."

I then reported to the Very Reverend Aloysius Grosse-Kappenberg, S.V.D., my Superior General and the Chancellor of Fu Jen University, that the one and only condition on which the Church had agreed to continue to subsidize Fu Jen, namely, the right to nominate a new Board of Trustees, had been rejected by the Ministry of Education of the "People's" government of China.

In a letter to my Superior General, shortly before this, I reduced and simplified the Fu Jen question. I wrote that the Church authorities must decide between one of two policies:

I. Continuing to finance Fu Jen, a center of atheism and marxist communism, in the hope of a change in the policy of the "People's" government of China, or else in the government itself, either of which would bring about a favourable change allowing the Church to carry on Fu Jen, at least as a neutral university, regarding religious matters.

II. Discontinuing the Church subsidy to Fu Jen because of its atheistic, communistic character.

Father Grosse-Kappenberg, S.V.D., submitted this question to the Congregation of the Propagation of the Faith which in turn submitted it to His Holiness, Pope Pius XII, for a decision.

His Holiness decided to discontinue the subsidy, thereby disassociating the Church from atheistic, communistic Fu Jen.

This action of mine in informing my Superiors about Fu Jen and about the decision of the Ministry of Education to allow the Church to finance Fu Jen without enjoying one iota of administrative control, was a "crime" of mine, opposing the progressive movement.

So I could go on, tiring the reader with a longer list of my alleged "crimes" against the "people" of China, but what has been stated here is enough to acquaint one with the kind of so-called "crimes" of which I was held guilty.

On October 12, 1950, Fu Jen was officially "taken over," better, confiscated or stolen, by the communist government of China.

On October 19, 1950, I received a cable from my Superior General in Rome, ordering me to return to the U.S.A.

On the following Monday, I applied for my exit permit. This was necessary in order to leave China.

Day after day, week after week, month after month, I called at the Bureau of Foreign Affairs of the Peking Police for my exit permit but was always told, it had not come through.

In the previous August 1950, I had applied for a renewal of my residential permit but this was denied me—I was not allowed to live in China.

So, from October 23, 1950 until my arrest, I was not allowed to live in China and I was denied the permission to leave China.

Such inconsistencies are common in communist China.

I was informed by a friend of mine in November, 1950, of a way of escaping from Red China. This friend gave the name, address and telephone number of a person, who could and would smuggle me out of China.

All I had to do was to present myself to this person, tell him my name and the name of my friend, and in an hour or so, I would be on my way out of communist China.

I thanked my friend for this kind offer but declined to avail myself of it.

This was because I wanted to wait until the release of Father Peter Huengsberg, S.V.D., of the Fu Jen University staff, who had been arrested on September 29, 1950. I expected him to be released any time, and I wanted to be around when he returned from prison so I could help him leave China.

Then, too, I thought that if I were smuggled out of China, all who knew me would be in danger of being punished by the communists.

As time went on, I was more and more avoided by those I knew, until finally, I was practically deserted by all.

No one visited me.

Hardly any one recognized me on the street.

Usually, if a Chinese who knew me, saw me coming, he or she turned and went in the opposite direction, or simply refused to look at me, on passing.

Friends and acquaintances destroyed all their photographs that featured me—destroyed all evidences, as letters, recommendations, books, indications of ever having known me, spoken to me or received any benefit from me.

I was abandoned.

Staff members and students of Fu Jen, many of whom I had helped, now turned against me, accused me to the police, requesting my arrest, in order to save themselves.

Yet, I understood and forgave them because I knew these good people were under great pressure at the hands of the communists, forcing them to act against their conscience.

I understood, better than before, how Our Blessed Lord must have suffered at His trial, when He saw the same people whom He had cured, consoled, preached to and those who had loudly hailed and welcomed Him, a few days before, on the First Palm Sunday, now joined in the mob, accusing Him of being a criminal, shouting to crucify Him!

As never before, I began to understand those unfathomable words of infinite charity and of boundless forgiveness! "Father, forgive them, for they do not know what they are doing." Luke XXIII, 34.

·5·

My Arrest

JULY 25, 1951, was a day when a decision was to be reached whether or not the cease-fire talks at Kaesong, Korea, were to be resumed. I had felt unwell and consequently taken a rather long rest after my noon dinner. At about 3:40 P.M., I arose, with the intention of listening in to the "Voice of America" broadcast at 4:00 o'clock, to learn whether or not the cease-fire talks in Korea were to be resumed.

As I started to dress, I was startled by the sound of many men running near my living-quarters. I looked up through a window and saw the top of a helmet dart by. Alarmed, I looked out of another window and saw many policemen in helmets with tommy guns surrounding my residence. A group of about six of them formed in a line, about 50 feet from the entrance of my residence, in battle formation, with their rifles pointed at the door and windows of my cabin-like residence. I then knew that what I had been expecting for twenty months, since the communist armies occupied Peiping, February 1, 1949, and especially for the last ten months, since the "People's" government of China had taken over Fu Jen University, was about to take place—I was to be arrested.

I dressed as fast as I could. A policeman looked in my bedroom and saw me. He then went to my door and beat on it demanding that I open it, which I did. In a moment my living quarters were filled with armed Sepo (Security Police). Two of them seized me by the arms while other policemen made a hurried search of my bedroom and toilet. As I had only my shorts, pants, shoes, and socks on, a shirt was quickly gotten from my bedroom and given to me to put on. A silver medal of the Blessed Virgin Mary on a silver chain, a gift of my brother, hanging around my neck, was taken off. I was then handcuffed with my hands behind my back. A policewoman showed me a cardlike paper and spoke in Chinese, then in English, saying, "You are arrested as an American spy." To this I could only wryly smile. Another policeman took my picture.

I was arrested!

My brain was flooded with thoughts and conjectures. I thought the Korean cease-fire talks had been called off, that a state of declared war existed between Red China and my country, the U.S.A., and as a consequence I was being arrested by the communists in retaliation against the U.S.A. I thought I might be taken out and shot as hundreds of Chinese had been since the beginning of the year. I also thought that I might be questioned and given rough treatment for a few hours or days and then deported, like other missionaries, as Bishop de Vienne of Tientsin. I was in a daze. I did not know what was in store for me.

I was then led out to the entrance of the compound where I lived, and ordered to stand there, facing a group of what seemed like 40 or 50 little children of the parish catechism school with their teacher. These little children knew me and loved me very much. Whenever they saw me, they would run up and surround me, holding my hands and arms, all laughing and talking at the same time.

Now it was so different!

These little creatures had evidently been drilled by the communist police to gather where they did and clap, approving my arrest. Children of lower primary school age, they were too young to hide their emotions.

I shall never forget that scene!

Handcuffed, I looked at them. Their little faces were distorted and torn by strong conflicting emotions: fear of the cruel communist police; love and sympathy for me, in chains. The poor little creatures were all crying. Some faintly clapped their little hands. Under inhuman pressure, they were forced to act against their finest, deepest, noblest sentiments. My brain was full of thoughts. I thought of what I had heard, how the Chinese communists had forced children to sign death petitions, requesting the execution of their fathers, and wives of their husbands. My heart went out to these tortured little children before me. Their evident sympathy for me consoled me. I blessed them, making a little sign of the cross with my right hand, handcuffed behind my back, and I thought that I needed no further proof or demonstration of the intrinsic malice of communism that so distorted, so twisted and so worked to destroy the finest, the noblest, the deepest sentiments in the hearts of little children!

My picture was taken again and I was then ordered onto a jeep, an American-made jeep, with 3 or 4 police guards. The rest of the Sepo boarded a truck. I was then driven in front of Fu Jen University, where all could see me in disgrace, in chains, being driven away by the dreaded Sepo. We turned south on the busy Hsi Szu Pai Lou Ta Chieh to the next street south of Hsi Szu Pai Lou, where we turned east to Ts'ao Lan Tzu Hutung, near the National Library. The jeep stopped at No. 13 of the hutung, before a high red gate and blew its horn, signaling to the guard to open the gate. As I looked at the gate, I thought of the words Dante placed over the gates of hell: "All hope abandon ye who enter here."

The gate slowly opened.

The jeep drove in. I was ordered out and placed in a little room. I wondered what was next. Was I to be shot? Was I to be deported immediately? Was I to be questioned then deported? In about 5 minutes a policeman came, removed my handcuffs and ordered me into a little nearby office where I was searched and my rosary, watch, fountain pen, Sheaffer pencil, knife and money were taken away from me. A list of these articles was then written up and I signed it first in English, then in Chinese. Lastly my finger print was added.

I was then led to a dark, damp corridor in an old one-story building, to Cell No. 10.

The heavy wooden door was opened with a clang of the iron bolt and I was ordered to enter. The door was then slammed and bolted with a bang.

I was in prison!

·6·

Cell No. 10

THE CELL WAS SMALL with a wooden kang (bed) in it. About six prisoners, all Chinese, were in the cell. In silence, they looked at me, then motioned me to sit down on the kang and one of them said in Chinese: "What is your name?"

"Rui Ko Ni," I replied, giving my name in Chinese.

"What is your nationality?"

"Mei Kuo jen (American)."

They then told me their names.

When I got over the first shock of being imprisoned, I looked around the cell. It was about 11 feet by 10 feet. The wall was white and bare. There was no clock or calendar. I thought of Robinson Crusoe who after being shipwrecked on an island, cut a notch in a tree everyday to keep a record of the passing days. Such I could not do, but I thought I would have to make a special effort to keep track of the days as they passed. A few days later, it became evident that this was unnecessary because when I was obliged to write statements or papers of my past activities, I could get the date for the paper from the chu chang or cell leader. In other cells a calendar was made each month by a cell-mate and pasted—usually with soap—on the wall.

The kang, about 6 feet by 10 feet and 18 inches high, was made of rough, wooden boards. The other cell mates had rolled up their thin cotton mattresses which were about one inch thick, and placed them against the wall.

There was one little window about 2 feet by 3 feet with

heavy iron bars. The floor was the bare ground; damp, black earth. In one corner of the cell was a hole in the earthen floor through which rats entered. There was another such hole under the kang. A strongly stinking wooden bucket was used as a urinal and in emergency cases for bowel movements. A single 15 candle power electric light was in the center of the ceiling. This burned all night. It was the only light for reading newspapers (always communist) when they were allowed and the other books of communist indoctrination. I wrote many papers in this poor light.

Under the kang were two bowls each about 18 inches wide. One was for drinking water which was issued hot or warm, and the other for food which was usually wo tou, an almost tasteless unleavened mixture of maize and water, which was steamed. Most prisoners had a little cup with a toothbrush for washing their teeth, and soap for washing their face and hands as well as for washing their clothes. These were kept under the kang. Most prisoners had a small bundle of clothes, usually a change in underwear and shirts. These were used as pillows.

The daily order in the cell was about as follows:

Rising at	6:15
Toilet	6:30
Study (brainwashing)	6:45
Breakfast	8:00
Study (brainwashing)	9:00
Free period	12:00
Study (brainwashing)	1:30
Supper	4:30
Toilet	5:15
Study (brainwashing)	7:00
Retiring	9:30

On Sundays the study periods after breakfast and before supper were dropped. Prisoners were free to sew clothes. Some, those making progress in being brainwashed, were allowed to play games as cards or other very simple games. For these games prisoners made cards of two or three sheets of paper pasted together with the figures drawn on them. Others made boards and pieces for various other games out of paper. Later, from 1953 on, a few prisoners bought manufactured playing cards and other games. A favorite card game was a kind of 500. Chinese chess was also played.

My imprisonment started about 5 P.M. o'clock. Prison supper was over. The cellmates asked me if I had eaten supper. I told them I had had a heavy noon dinner and was not hungry. The events of the afternoon spoilt whatever appetite I could have had.

I sat on the edge of the kang, next to the wall. One cell-mate who knew a little English told me that all the cell-mates were spies, friends of Truman, the President of the USA, whom the communists had stigmatized as the enemy of the Chinese "people."

I suspected that one or all of the cell-mates were Sepo, planted in the cell to observe me. Later I discarded this idea. I soon got the idea that the Sepo need not plant any of their members in the cells because the cell-mates with few exceptions were all anxious to demonstrate how they had changed from being anti-communist, Kuomintang (KMT) or American agents, to pro-communists, by co-operating with the prison authorities whenever and however possible. They readily and vehemently joined in tou chengs.

A "tou cheng (accusation process)" consisted of many gathering around a prisoner, shouting at him, cursing him, insulting him, pointing fingers at him, while he usually stood with head down. It was a nerve racking procedure. Often a tou cheng lasted for hours. It was dreaded by all prisoners. Few could stand it very long. It was commonly employed to force a fellow prisoner to confess crimes or reveal his thoughts.

A pro-communist attitude was also shown by watching closely other cell-mates for infractions of the prison rules or for other reactionary indications, all of which would usually be religiously reported to the chu chang to be relayed by him to the officer.

Hence, the Sepo had many informers, many "running dogs" as the Chinese call such characters, many pro-communist activists among the prisoners. The Sepo need not use their own members or agents to watch or spy on prisoners or to lead in the tou chengs. The prisoners themselves supplied these.

The communists turned the prisoners on themselves, used prisoners arrested as reactionaries, to punish or work on other prisoners also arrested as reactionaries. The communist policy of sowing discord and division amongst their enemies obtained even in prison.

At 9:45 P.M. the signal for retirement was given by an officer blowing a whistle and shouting "shui, chao! (sleep)."

In a moment's time, all the cell was in activity. The other cell mates quickly put away their books, unrolled their mattresses, took off their shirts and pants and lay down. I was impressed by the speed and uniformity of action. No one delayed. No one was at a loss what to do.

I had no mattress, no covering for the cool of the evening. I saw a coat hanging on the wall and indicated that I would like to use it as a cover, but the cell-mates forbade me to touch it. It was against the rules to use others' belongings as I learned later; the permission of the chu chang was necessary for such and my chu chang offered no such permission.

So I lay on the hard wooden kang in a place allotted me by the chu chang, next to the wall. All seven of us lay down on the kang about 10 feet wide.

The light was not turned off. It was kept burning. This was the policy throughout my prison experience. When the electric current was cut off for one reason or the other, a lit candle was brought into the cell.

· 7 ·

My First Court Session

I LAY DOWN for my first night in prison. After about fifteen minutes, I heard the loud and chilling clanging of the bolted lock of my cell door. The door opened and an officer called "Rui Ko Ni!"

I arose, the officer approached and asked if I were Rui Ko Ni, to which I replied, "Yes."

He then motioned me to leave the cell. I started to put on my shoes and the other cell-mates began to shout, "Kuai! Kuai! (Hurry! Hurry!)." They lost no opportunity to demonstrate to the officer how much a group of activists they had become. I tried to lace my low top shoes but the cell-mates hurried me and a few pushed me out.

I left the cell followed by the officer. Outside the building was a soldier with a drawn pistol. I had never seen such a big pistol. It looked like a big automatic 45, but longer and larger than any I had ever seen. The officer handed me over to the Sepo guard who shouted at me to walk towards the entrance of the prison compound, ahead of him. He shouted, "Kuai! Kuai!"

It was dark. As I passed through the entrance of the compound, I came into open ground. I could not see anything beyond my immediate surroundings of about ten feet.

I hesitated, not knowing in which direction to proceed, and feared that I might be tricked by my guard to walk into the open to be shot by another for attempting to escape. My guard was angered by my hesitation and shouted: "Tsou! Tsou! Kuai! Kuai! (Go! Go! Quick! Quick!)."

I proceeded not knowing what to expect or whither I was going. The guard pointed the direction to go and followed close after me with his drawn pistol pointed at me and his index finger dangerously near the trigger. This was the usual manner the Sepo guards observed in taking a prisoner from place to place.

After walking about 300 feet and making several turns, I arrived before a row of rooms in a long, one storied building. The guard ordered me to halt, then shouted, announcing that he had arrived with me. I heard a reply, "Lai! (Come in!)." The guard then shouted at me to enter the door before which we stood. I entered and found myself in Court Room No. 4 of the "People's" Military Court.

The court room was about 18 feet wide by about 27 feet long. At one end was the judge sitting at a desk, the size and shape of an ordinary office desk. To his right, at another such desk sat the recorder, who took down in Chinese the minutes, including the statements of the judge and prisoner. To the left of the judge sat, in my case, the interpreter at a desk similar to that of the judge.

In front of the judge, to his left, near the wall, sat the guard with his pistol drawn and his finger near the trigger of his pistol which he pointed to the concrete floor at my feet. To the rear of the judge and to his right was a cabinet in which were kept court records.

On the wall, to the rear and above the judge, was a picture of the greatest quisling of history, the man who betrayed 600,000,000 Chinese, his fellow countrymen, to the Soviet Union: Chairman Mao Tse-tung.

I was ordered by the Sepo guard to stand before a wooden chair facing the judge, with my face about half a foot from an electric light hung from the wall and surrounded by swarms of insects that soon began to torment me by crawling over my face, head and neck and some biting me. I was forbidden to scatter these pests away with a slap or waving of my hand. The light, moreover, so near me, pained my eyes. The Sepo guard seized my spectacles and jerked them off, throwing them on a nearby window sill. The judge, a thin, lean man, who looked about 30 years old, eyed me for a minute or so then ordered me to sit down. He spoke in Chinese. I spoke in English. An interpreter translated for us.

I sat down.

"What is your name?"

"Rigney, in English; Rui Ko Ni, in Chinese," I replied.

"What is your full name?"

"Harold William Rigney."

"Where do you live?"

"Li Kwang Chiao, Nan Chieh, No. 1."

"What is your nationality?"

"American."

"What is your occupation?"

"I am a Catholic priest, a missionary, the rector of Fu Jen University."

"Now, tell me what crimes you have committed against the Chinese 'people.' "

"I have committed no crimes against the Chinese people."

"SHIH MA! (WHAT!)" he shouted at the top of his voice as he banged his fist on his desk.

"CHAN CHI LAI! (Stand up!)"

I stood up. My head was soon surrounded by the swarm of insects around the lamp and the glare of the electric light was painful.

So started my trial that was to last three years and two months.

The first phase of this ordeal lasted about sixty days and nights. In the early part of this phase, the first week of my trial, I stated clearly and emphatically, "I am a Catholic and

I will not give up my religion; I would rather die. Moreover, I will not become a communist." The judge replied, "No one asks you to give up your religion and you could not become a communist even if you wanted to."

During this period of the first sixty days and nights, I was allowed only two nights of rest. One was when I had a fever with chills and the prison physician prescribed a night of rest. The other was granted me by the judge with the evident purpose of letting me realize how sweet a night's rest was, even on boards, although I was tortured throughout the night whenever I awoke with the dread that I would be called out to court.

During this period, every night, I had one or two court sessions from around bed time to after day break. A few times, especially towards the end, I was allowed one or two hours of sleep in the morning, before and during day-break. If I had one session, it continued uninterrupted from bed time to day-break or after. If I had two sessions, the first ended around mid-night and the second began around one or two o'clock. During the break of one or two hours, I either was ordered by the judge to sit on a rock or on the ground in the drill grounds with a Sepo guard nearby or I was sent back to my wretched cell to sit up, without sleeping. In either case I was ordered to think over certain "crimes" I was supposed to have committed or to examine my mind or conscience to bring to memory or to move my will to recognize or admit "crimes."

As a rule, I spent this time in earnest prayer.

I usually had one or two court sessions during the day: during the late morning and the late afternoon or just one of these periods. I think I had about 150 court sessions during this period of 60 days and 60 nights.

They were terrible nights and days!

·8·

Wo Tou and Pai Tsai

I GRADUALLY WORE AWAY, becoming very thin. I was fat at the time of my arrest, weighing 180 pounds which is much since I am small boned. In the first weeks in prison, I dropped to less than 100 pounds. I was very hungry since I could not eat the food served me. The pigs in America eat better than I did. Our regular food was wo tou and pai tsai.

"Wo tou" was three or four ounces of a poor grade of corn meal, compared to American standards. This was mixed with water without salt or any leaven as yeast or baking soda, shaped like a thimble and steamed. One bite and I lost my appetite. It took me about four months to get used to it and eat enough to stave off hunger for an hour or two. During these early months, evidently to keep me alive, I was given saltless, tasteless boiled rice which I could eat, along with a little wo tou.

"Pai tsai" was boiled water with a little Chinese cabbage in it. To call this soup would be misleading, since soup according to our idea must contain some meat or fish. I liked the pai tsai, but for the first three months I was given from one-third to one-half a bowl of it, while the other prisoners received a full bowl. A bowl held about three quarters of a pint of liquid. There was no evident reason for reducing the one item of food I could easily take, unless it was a scheme to starve or undernourish me.

We ate twice a day, in late morning and late afternoon. By night I was very hungry.

Throughout my imprisonment in Ts'ao Lan Tzu, we were served special meals about 12 times a year. We prisoners looked forward to these meals weeks in advance and ate them like hungry dogs, eating as fast as possible—they tasted so good! These special meals consisted of Kan Fan (dry, steamed rice) or man tou (Chinese steamed wheat flour bread) with meat soup. The meat was cut to the size of bouillon cubes and each prisoner received 3 or 4 of these pieces, or none at all. In my first year in prison, I think I had received from the government at the most 3 or 4 ounces of meat.

How I longed for a good meal!

How I longed for salt! I was salt-starved. Our food was deficient in this very important element of diet. Most of the prisoners had their own private supply of salt, which they had either purchased or had sent to them by relatives. I was not allowed to purchase salt. Neither was I allowed to receive any kinds of supplies, food or clothing, from the outside.

A cell-mate who was quite decent, had some salt which he had purchased. Each afternoon when hot drinking water was issued to us, he would put a big pinch of salt in his wan or bowl of water. I used to watch him and long for a pinch. One day when no one was looking, I asked him to please give me a pinch of salt. He did, putting it in my bowl of water.

My! how delicious the water tasted!

I still feel grateful to this kind young man for his real charity and would like to meet him someday to thank him and make returns for that pinch of salt.

About a week later, I asked him again for a pinch of salt but he refused. I thought he refused because his stock of salt was down and I felt no resentment towards him. Later I learned it was against the rule to give anything to a fellow prisoner without permission of the chu chang or cell leader since giving things was an imperialistic way to make friends, and friendship between cell-mates was strictly forbidden and the taboo was rigidly enforced. Hell is like this. There are no friendships there.

During the first year in prison I considered the most important item to purchase or have sent by relatives or friends was salt. Next in order of importance was toilet paper and then soap for toilet and laundry uses.

For toilet paper, a rough kind of paper about a foot and a half by two feet and a half was obtained and torn into pieces about 2½ inches by 4 inches.

The government supplied toilet paper and soap only to those prisoners who could not purchase them—either because they had no money on hand or lacked permission to buy anything—or else failed to receive supplies from outside the prison—either because no one had the courage to send them needed supplies, or permission to secure such was denied them by the government.

Those prisoners who depended on the communist government of China for such necessities as toilet paper and soap were pitiable indeed. The supplies they received from the government were inadequate, consequently they kept their eyes open for scraps of paper of any kind, that could be used for toilet paper. If they saw any, they snatched it up for future use. They also were on the alert for used laundry water with a heavy amount of suds. This they used to wash their clothes.

I was allowed after a month or so in prison to buy toilet paper and soap. The rats, however, ate the soap in a day's time and for about four months I washed my face and hands as well as handkerchiefs in cold water without soap.

My first morning in prison was spent in a court session that lasted until long after day break. I returned from court to my cell after the time for rising. I was very tired from the first night's ordeal and lay down on the wooden kang to rest and sleep. The cell-mates soon swarmed around me, telling me it was forbidden to sleep during the day time.

It was one of the first mornings in prison that I washed my face for the first time. I had returned from the court early enough to get a short sleep of about an hour or so. When the signal for rising was given, everybody jumped up, dressed and began to wash.

The chu chang washed first in about a pint of water, washing his face and hands; then others followed.

I was last.

The water was full of dirt, etc. from the face and hands of six cell-mates.

I objected to washing in this and tried to explain the utter unsanitary nature of me using such water. I told the cell-mates that certain eye diseases were common in China and that the Chinese were completely or partially immune to them but foreigners like me were not. This only brought me much abuse from the cell-mates who insisted from then on that I should wash last, using their dirty water. In a few days, my eyes were bloodshot from an infection of some sort for which I received no medical care.

Bodily Filth, Lice and Intelligence Work

JULY AND AUGUST are hot and humid days in Peking. I was arrested on July 25th, 1951, in the midst of the hot season. In my living quarters at Fu Jen, I bathed two or three times a day—on rising, on retiring and usually in the late afternoon.

In prison it was otherwise. During the hot season and autumn, from July 25th, to around mid-November, I had in all only two or three sponge baths in my cell with about one quart of cold water. I was allowed no better opportunities to bathe. My first hot bath was in mid-November. During this time the residue of perspiration and dirt—and Peking is notorious for its dust—accumulated on me.

I was wretched.

I often requested the court to allow me a hot bath but was always told that I had to confess first.

The cell-mates heaped insults on me, telling me that I gave off a disagreeable body odor, instead of reporting this to the chu chang with the intention of him arranging that I take a hot bath.

One day, the chu chang shouted at me that he could smell me, and that this was very disagreeable to him. He then ordered me to sit in the corner as far as possible from him.

On such occasions I replied that all I needed was a hot bath.

Before long I was full of lice. Most of the prisoners had lice, which they picked up in prison if they did not have them before their arrest.

Later, when the communists accused the Americans of

carrying on germ warfare in Korea, whenever a cell-mate found lice on himself, he usually pointed to me saying words such as: "These came from that American imperialist." My reply, whenever I gave one, was that I had no lice when I entered prison.

Later, searching for lice on one's clothing became a daily routine. Each prisoner undressed, thoroughly examining his various items of clothing for vermin. In the winter time, when the cells were cold, prisoners covered their unclothed bodies with their short cotton coats (mien aou). I always felt relieved when I discovered and killed any of these insects. The more I found, the more relieved I felt. The most lice I ever found in one search were nine. I became quite expert in the technique of lice hunting.

That such an occupation could be a mental relief is an indication of the dullness of the prison life at Ts'ao Lan Tzu.

During the first days of my court sessions, the judge insisted that I was a spy.

I denied this. At one of the sessions of the early part of my trial, the time of which I do not remember, the judge informed me that in one of my monthly reports to my Superior General in Rome, I gave the price of millet or hsiao mi, the staple food of North China. This was economic intelligence, he said, which was as important as military intelligence.

He added that it was this economic intelligence that I gave to the Vatican and America, that was responsible for the economic embargo Washington placed on China.

So he was holding me responsible for the economic embargo which was doing so much harm to the economics of China.

I tried to explain that I reported to my Superior General the price of millet at times of crises, in the past inflation, when prices of commodities sky-rocketed, in order to explain why we at Fu Jen increased salaries, to keep up with the cost of living. In the early year of the communist occupation salaries were reckoned in terms of catties or pounds of millet.

The judge became very angry and said I was arguing and that I was not allowed to argue but only to confess my crimes, accuse myself and others.

I sent my monthly reports to my Superior General, copies of which were sent to Father Ralph of Chicago, Illinois, by mail from Peking, or by travellers leaving China for Hong Kong where Father Joseph Henkels, S.V.D., forwarded them on to their destination.

On one occasion a friend who was leaving Tientsin by ship for Hong Kong took two monthly reports of mine to be delivered to Father Henkels in Hong Kong for remailing. This person was searched by a customs officer who found and confiscated these reports. The customs officer assured this person the reports would be returned in a few days.

But the days and weeks passed, and no reports were ever returned.

The judge then told me what I am certain was another lie, namely that the court had all these monthly reports of mine to Rome and Chicago and that I could not hide anything from the court but would be forced to confess everything about them. If I failed to confess any item of these reports, the court would know that I was dishonest.

He then emphasized that my reports contained economic intelligence.

After about three or four days I said that if the communist government considered this as intelligence work, inquiring about the price of millet from the market reports in the newspaper and informing others about it, then I did do intelligence work, but I was not a professional spy.

This angered him and he pounded the desk shouting that I was a spy and that was all there was to it.

I then spent about two weeks of court sessions of night and day, about forty sessions in all, confessing the contents of my monthly reports in my efforts to prevent strikes at Fu Jen, which were called acts of sabotaging of the progressive movement; the Survey of the Church of North China, which I had conducted and was considered a "crime" according to the communists; as well as the rumors I had relayed to my O.S.S. friend and the U. S. Consulate friends. After these sessions, I told the judge I had no more to confess.

·10·

Condemned to Death

W<small>HEN</small> I <small>TOLD</small> the judge I had no more to confess, he became furious, pounded on his desk and shouted: "Are you an O.S.S. agent or a State Department agent?"

"I am an agent of neither, although I reported intelligence to them as I have confessed," I replied.

He then ordered the Sepo guard to put fetters, which were at hand, on me.

The guard ordered me to sit on the cement floor with my legs stretched out. He then proceeded to place these fetters which were of rough, rusty, dirty iron on me. He fastened them with an iron bolt that he hammered tight with a heavy hammer making loud, dull, bangs.

The judge then ordered the guard to take me to the drill grounds where I was obliged to walk up and down for what seemed like about fifteen minutes until my ankles were raw and bleeding from the fetters. I was then returned to the court and ordered to stand at attention before the judge.

He looked at me and repeated his question, "Are you an O.S.S. agent or a State Department agent?"

"I am an agent of neither, though I gave intelligence to them as I have admitted," I replied.

The judge banged his desk and ordered me handcuffed.

The Sepo guard seized my hands and as roughly as he could, handcuffed them behind my back. There was no chain between each cuff, so that my wrists almost touched. The handcuffs were rough, rusty and dirty and in a day or so cut into my skin.

The judge then eyed me and shouted again: "Are you an O.S.S. agent or a State Department agent?"

"I am neither, although I gave intelligence to them as I have confessed," I replied again for the third time.

The judge then took a sheet of paper, about the size of typewriting paper and wrote on it, as though he were signing it, and looking at me with a steady, cool look said, "You are condemned to death!"

I was stunned but calm.

I looked at the judge, the recorder and the interpreter and hoped that one day one of them would leave the evil path of communism and tell the truth about me: that I had been falsely accused of being a spy and had been shot because I had refused to make a false confession.

Therefore, to make a formal declaration that the various members of the court could note and remember, I said, "I die a martyr of truth."

"You die an imperialist spy."

The judge motioned me to leave the court room.

I slowly walked to the door, dragging my fetter chains on the floor. The pain of the fetters was unnoticed by me, crowded out of my mind by the thought of my approaching death.

As I reached the door, I stopped. The interpreter rushed to my side. "Ah! Rui Ko Ni is breaking, he wants to confess," he must have thought.

But I turned to the judge and said, "Since I am going to die, I want a priest. I am a Catholic and we Catholics want a priest before we die. You say you guarantee freedom of religion, therefore you must allow me to see a priest."

"There is no time for such! Get out of here!"

As I left the court, I heard a bugle blow and saw a number of military guards rush out of their barracks.

"These are the firing squad," I thought.

With the armed guard at my rear, I slowly walked towards the drill grounds, to die.

I felt the bullets of the firing squad piercing my chest and heart, as I thought I would die standing before a firing squad rather than the traditional way of kneeling down and being shot in the back of the head by one bullet.

I said my final act of contrition and offered my life for the conversion of China, as well as for the eternal salvation of my near relatives, the spiritual and temporal welfare of all my relatives, benefactors and friends and lastly for the spiritual welfare of my persecutors.

My mind was preoccupied with these thoughts and prayers. I regarded little of my surroundings.

I felt a deep sense of peace and even joy at the thought that as a missionary, bearing testimony to Christ, I was to die a martyr as countless missionaries and apostles before me had! I had read much about these heroes who died for Christian virtue: usually faith. Now I was to join this noble group! a martyr for another Christian virtue: the truth.

God knew I was dying a martyr. The world might be deceived by the lies of my communist executioners and consider I died a spy. Perhaps my friends might never know or even believe that I died a martyr but God would, and that was all that mattered. God and my soul were all that counted then and my martyrdom was being offered for those who would perhaps pass me off as a priest, a missionary, untrue to his calling, who engaged in spying and was executed for such crimes.

So I trudged on, handcuffed and in fetters.

I reached the drill grounds and looked around and noted that on two sides were bare walls, while the other two sides were open.

I did not know before which wall I should stand to face the firing squad and be shot.

Stopping I turned to my guard for instructions as to which wall to proceed. The guard became angry and shouted, "Tsou! Tsou! (Go! Go!)"

"Well," I thought, "I am not to die now but later, most likely this afternoon." I recalled that since the beginning of 1951, hundreds of others had died in Peking, being shot in the afternoon, at the Tien Ch'iao (Bridge of Heaven).

The Tien Ch'iao was in the southern city of Peking near Tien Tan (Temple of Heaven). Condemned prisoners, bound hand and foot, with a strip of paper on their back, at right angles like a long fin, with their crimes written on it, were driven on trucks around Peking, through the most crowded streets as Wang Fu Ching Ta Chieh (Morrison Street), so the terrorized people could see them and learn what was the fate of those who dared oppose the communist government of Mao Tse-tung.

These poor creatures were then driven to the Tien Ch'iao roughly, and cruelly moved or thrown from the truck. Each was ordered to kneel down while the Sepo executioner, brandishing his rifle, to express his delight in murdering a "criminal" and "enemy of the 'people'," got behind the bent figure, took aim at the back of his head, and fired.

On one occasion a friend of mine saw a truck of condemned prisoners being driven down Wang Fu Ching Ta Chieh. To the rear of each condemned prisoner was a Sepo guard. One courageous prisoner shouted "Wan Sui, Chiang Chieh Shih (Long live Chiang Kai Shek)." The cruel brute of a communist soldier, a Sepo guard, behind him, became furious. He beat the condemned patriot over the head with the butt of his rifle, then gagged him so he could speak no more.

The onlooking people, already terrorized, were horrified by this beastliness.

·11·

Cell-Mates and the Communists'
Court Procedure

As SOON AS I entered the cell, with my hands handcuffed behind me and in fetters, the cell-mates began to shout abusive language at me and quickly surrounded me. They forced me to kneel on the ground. I feared one would get behind me and push me forward on my face. I would be unable to prevent this if it were attempted. So I managed to move nearer a wall with my back as close to it as possible to prevent any one from getting behind me.

The cell-mates demanded that I speak Chinese. They claimed I could speak Chinese and only pretended to be unable to do so. They pushed me from one to the other, shouting all the while, as I was knocked from side to side, back and forth like a cork tumbler or what the Chinese call a pu tao weng. I said just about all the Chinese I knew, with my poor pronunciation and disregard of tones. The cell-mates shouted that I could speak Chinese and should say more. I repeated what I had said over and over again.

It should have been evident to anyone whose mother tongue was Chinese that I was unable to speak their language.

One cell-mate, an elderly Manchu physician of seventy-two years of age, sat in his place, declining to join in torturing me. Soon the chu chang turned on him and ordered him to participate in the tou cheng. The elderly gentleman, for such he was, every inch of him, slowly shifted himself until he came to the edge of the kang and started to reprimand me in tones and in a manner that it was evident to me that he was in full sympathy for me. He was obliged to say something by way of a reprimand or else undergo torture and the poor old gentleman was daily suffering plenty of that at the hands of the rest of the cellmates who proved themselves to be "running dogs" of the communists.

This went on for one, two or three hours. I do not remember. It is strange how one can be tortured for a long time and lose the sense of the duration of the torture.

The mockery was brought to a stop when I was called to court.

When the court session opened, it was evident from the questions of the judge that I was not to be shot soon. The death sentence he had passed on me a few hours previously was only a bluff, another deception, one more lie, of "the children of darkness," to trick me into a confession. Evidently the judge hoped that when he condemned me to death, I would fall on my knees, beg for my life, buy my life by confessing falsely that I was a spy, an agent of either the O.S.S. or the State Department. But I did not do this. His treachery failed.

The bugle I had heard and the armed soldiers I had seen leaving their barracks, in the early morning when I left the court expecting to be shot, was simply the changing of the guard and not the assembling of an execution squad, as I had thought.

At almost every court session after this for two years, the judge threatened to shoot me. He did this so often that it soon little bothered me. He wanted to shoot me, of this I have little doubt, but his decision or wish was not final.

Once during these first sixty days, he told me, with his face contorted with hatred, that he could kill me with the same eagerness and lack of compassion that he had when killing a fly.

So spoke a judge of the communist military court, a judge who is obliged by tradition, professional ethics, and the laws of civilized governments to take an impassionate attitude, an unprejudiced view towards a prisoner being tried!

"In the 'people's democracies,' court procedure is different from that in the 'imperialist' countries," I was told over and over again with long and full explanations by my judge, chu changs and cell-mates.

In the courts of the "imperialist" countries, prisoners are punished for what they confess, not for what they do not confess.

On the other hand, in the courts of the "people's democracies" as here in the "people's" China, prisoners are punished not for what they confess but for what they do not confess. The procedure is so simple, so human! Just confess your crimes and you will be forgiven! No one is clearly told what crimes he is charged with, either at the time of his arrest or during his trial. But he must confess the crimes he is charged with.

As a consequence, almost every prisoner in Ts'ao Lan Tzu, especially in 1951 and 1952, embarked on a program of confessing every possible crime he ever committed or could have committed. He exaggerated his past activities, minor offenses or peccadilloes into grave and huge crimes. He often multiplied these. This was done in the hope of confessing the crimes listed against him and also to demonstrate how tender his conscience had become, how much he now looked at his past in the light of the "people," in the hope of saving his life, or receiving a lighter sentence or even of being released.

Some prisoners even falsely confessed that they had committed one or more murders.

The elderly Manchu physician, mentioned above, made about one hundred false confessions, under torture of the cell-mates, and in the hope of satisfying the court. The cell-mates, running dogs of the communists, would tou cheng the elderly gentleman of seventy-two, this first-class Chinese scholar of the old type, subjecting him to various tortures.

I remember once when I returned from a court session, the elderly gentleman was passing through one of these ordeals.

He was standing up with extended arms, near the stinking urine bucket, while the other cell-mates proceeded with their discussion of the study matter. Whenever the elderly gentleman even budged, they shouted and abused him. Finally the old man could stand it no longer and collapsed. He was then hauled up and thrown on the kang to revive as best his advanced years and declining physiological powers allowed him to, so he could be further tortured.

He won relief only when he indicated his willingness to confess and confessed something. After a short respite of a few hours or a day, when his confession was declared inadequate by his judge, he would be subjected to more tortures. This went on for about half a year, during which time I was moved four times, and was told by my new chu chang that the elderly Manchu had eventually fully confessed. He was then sentenced.

I fear this venerable man is still rotting in one of the many prisons of Peking, serving a long sentence, making match boxes or the like.

Around the beginning of 1953, the prison officers changed their tune and of course the chu chang followed suit. We were told that there were two elements in the treatment of our crimes. One was clemency granted for full, complete confession accompanied with reformation. This had been over-emphasized in the past. The other element which had been ignored by the prisoners, we were told, was expiation of crimes—the sentences.

So, after tricking the average prisoner into accusing himself of crimes, real or fictitious, known or unknown to the court, they sentence him, according to the evidence they have, to serve a term, based on his confessed crimes, some of which the court first learned about from the prisoner's confession.

Another characteristic of the court procedure of communist China is the deprivation of advisors whom a prisoner can trust.

A prisoner on being arrested is locked up, held incommunicado, deprived of calling a lawyer for advice. He is allowed no counsel. He is tortured, pressed, cajoled, tricked into a confession. The judge is supposed to be the friend and advisor of the prisoner.

So a person in the communist China I know, is guilty on being arrested of crimes of which he is not made acquainted by the court. He has no counsel; is forbidden a counsel and prevented from having one. He is not allowed to defend himself, to explain any of his conduct of the past which might be presented as evidence of crimes. He is not allowed to deny the crimes for which he was arrested—such a denial would be an additional crime. He is allowed only to accuse himself and others; to confess his crimes and implicate others. This cruel mockery is called justice, communist justice.

I often wondered how many unfortunate men and women, Chinese and foreign, of China, have been executed or are serving long sentences for no other reason than that they refused to admit crimes they never committed!

Prisoner Wang was an English speaking Chinese cell-mate who had studied in the U.S.A. He had been a businessman with many American connections. He was a likable person with a pleasant personality, and had first been assigned to "help" me after I had been arrested only about a week or ten days. He pressed me to confess I was an American agent. He never once advised me to tell the truth. He dinned in my ear day after day, week after week, month after month, that I should confess I was an American agent, an O.S.S. or an F.B.I. man, and stick to it, and I would soon be deported. He

53

was fundamentally a kind man but he could and did abuse me much. He hoped to win his release over my dead or long-imprisoned body, inducing me to confess truthfully or falsely, that I was an American agent. Yet, I understood and forgave him. His wife, he said, had died just three months before his arrest, leaving six children, ranging from a baby to a nineteen-year-old daughter. Wang was doing his best to get free to return to his motherless children.

The court knew from the confession of a Chinese prisoner who had been employed by O.S.S., with the rank of a colonel, that I had known some O.S.S. personnel, had searched Fu Jen for a radio of the former German Embassy, and had told O.S.S. about rumors concerning the communist army near Peiping.

I had become acquainted with O.S.S. personnel in the U. S. Army Airbase, Accra, Gold Coast, when an officer of this branch of the army approached me asking me to help in a marriage case, in which no collecting of intelligence was involved. He asked my assistance to prevent a marriage between an American of the U. S. Army and a suspected Nazi, who was further suspected of trying to gain admission into the U. S. by marrying an American.

I also spoke to these O.S.S. personnel about local Gold Coast geography and tribes as well as personalities.

In Tunis, I also knew a few of the O.S.S. personnel.

Wang, who had been instructed by the judge regarding me, insisted that my connection with O.S.S. in Peking classified me an O.S.S. "Formal enrollment and reception of a salary are not needed for one to officially become a member of the O.S.S.," he explained, according to communist standards.

Hence, I finally said, "From this point of view, I am an O.S.S."

In the subsequent court session, the judge asked me where I joined, how did I apply for membership, what kind of training did I receive, etc.

After a few minutes of this, I said, "Well, judge, if you ?
that being an O.S.S. involves all this, then I am no O.?
never joined the O.S.S. or received training from them. I ?
some O.S.S. and relayed rumors to them but that was a?
connections with them."

At that the judge became very angry, shouting at ?
pounding on his desk, reprimanding and cursing me, ca?
me a guttersnipe, a shameless, cunning spy, etc. But I ?
to this denial.

12

Confessions of a Sleeping Prisoner

As I STATED above, during my first sixty days and nights of imprisonment, I had two full nights of rest. In the latter part of these days, my physical reserves were at an end.

I was subjected to the nerve racking of long court sessions during the night as well as the day. I was exhausted from lack of sleep. I was tortured by a gnawing hunger, I was covered with bodily dirt and weeks of unwashed perspiration. My one and only set of clothes, that were literally falling to shreds, were infested with lice. My ankles and wrists, sore and bleeding from the fetters and handcuffs I wore, were in extreme pain. My legs and arms were swollen from these shackles. Often, especially in the long night court sessions when I perspired profusely, I was tormented by thirst. I had never cared much for tea, but often as I was plagued by thirst, as the judge quaffed cup after cup of tea, serving himself and the recorder and interpreter, my mouth watered in vain, for a cup of tea. I thought that if I ever would become a free man again, I would drink tea, a gallon of tea. I had been subjected to endless humiliation and insults.

In this state of wretchedness I was called out of my cell one night around 9:45 P.M., the time for retiring. There was nothing unusual about such a call. But this call opened up an unusual experience for me, unusual even for my Ts'ao Lan Tzu experiences.

The Sepo guard directed me to a room in a courtyard adjoining the court rooms.

The male interpreter was there. He told me to sit on a soft sofa. This was unusual treatment—apparent kindness. He then began to talk to me in soft, unctuous words, explaining how I could help myself by confessing my crimes. Such would lead to clemency on the part of the government. The court had dealt harshly, it is true, with me, he explained, but I would experience a bountiful generosity on the part of the government if I would only confess. It would not take long, only about an hour of confessing to clear up my case. Why be so obstinate? The government did not want me to suffer but to enjoy life. I was only harming myself by being stubborn, preventing the government from showing how benevolent it could be.

So he went on for about one hour. I, struggling to keep awake, told him I would like to clear up my case but I had no crimes to confess.

He was a little ruffled by this but continued his cajoling line. I was favorably impressed by his "kindness."

I was then led to the court room and told to sit down.

This was unusual.

Formerly, for weeks, I was obliged to stand at attention during my court sessions. This night, however, the judge magnanimously told me to sit down.

I saw cats and dogs running all over the court room. Cats were jumping in and out of the waste paper basket at the side of the judge. After a few questions put to me by the judge, my delirious brain could fully function no more.

I went to sleep.

All I remember is that I said, "Yes" to many questions the judge put to me. How long this went on, I do not remember. It stretched out into the hours.

Finally, I came to.

I opened my heavy eyes and raised my nodding head to look at the judge and the cats I saw jumping in and out of his waste paper basket.

57

A fear suddenly came over me. "I have admitted too much. I have confessed too much," I thought.

Then I said, "What I have said tonight must not be taken as true and valid unless I confirm it."

The judge called the session ended and ordered me to return to my cell.

As I arose and walked to the door, dragging along my fetters with my hands handcuffed behind my back, the interpreter quickly picked up the red fingerprint ink pad, seized my right index finger, rubbed red ink on it and pressed to this finger the lower right hand part of the paper with the questions of the night put to me by the judge and my answers.

My fingerprint was on this paper. Whatever I had said that evening was unsigned but bore my fingerprint forced from shackled hands. It made an impressive document for an international court, or for one of the deluded or deluding communist sympathizers from the western world, (many of whom wear the garb of a clergyman, or carry the title of a barrister at law, a scientist, a politician), visiting Peking.

I was much disturbed by this forcing a fingerprint from me. I was certain I had incriminated myself, while I slept from sheer exhaustion or had been put into a trance.

The "kindness" of the interpreter and the judge were only deceptions of cunning communist court officials to trick me into a false confession. I knew from past experiences and reliable testimony that communists are never to be trusted. Their words mean nothing. Only their deeds can be accepted. Yet, I had given them my confidence, in a sleeping condition, and I feared they had led me into a false confession.

The judge opened my next session on the following night with words like these: "Last night you confessed very well. You were honest for a change. You confessed that you led a conspiracy to assassinate Chairman Mao Tse-tung. This is the most serious crime committed in China since the liberation.

This is the one crime for which the government refuses to grant clemency. You shall be shot. You cannot be pardoned or have your death sentence commuted. Now, show your good attitude and help the government by confessing all our leaders whom you planned to assassinate, who your leader in this plot was; who your co-conspirators were and who were under you. If you help the government in this way, you shall not be shot immediately, but after a time."

I was dumbfounded.

My head began to swim.

It seemed the court room changed. I always think of the court room as having curtains hung from the ceiling on either side of the judge on that night.

I told the judge I never heard of this plot until days after it was to have been committed, October 1st, 1950. He said this could not be true since the police had never released the news about this plot, whereas I had spoken about it a few nights previously at a dinner in the British Embassy. To this I replied that I had heard of this plot from a speech Ch'en Yuan, the Chinese president of Fu Jen University, had given at Fu Jen University. Ch'en Yuan warned the staff and student body of Fu Jen to beware of conspirators, that there had been a plot to murder Mao Tse-tung by a shell fired at him from a trench mortar as he reviewed, on the Tien An Men, the October 1st parade. He further stated that two foreigners, Riva, an Italian, and Yamaguchi, a Japanese, were to be executed as important members of this plot, but they would not be executed immediately.

I then continued that nowhere in the civilized world is the testimony of a drunken or sleeping man accepted as valid and stated that last night I was asleep when I confessed this.

After repeating this several times, I proceeded to the third point in my fight to save my life.

"I am your prisoner," I said. "My feet are fettered and my hands are handcuffed. I am helpless. You can shoot me if you want. I can do nothing. But," I continued, "if you shoot me, the man you want would still be at large. I am not the man you want."

Throughout that hectic night, I hammered at the last two points: "I was asleep, consequently my confession is invalid and I am not the man you want."

The judge all the while insisted that the court had its own evidence of my guilt in this matter. I should stop my arguing, stop defending myself and confess, show my good attitude, my willingness to help the government by confessing and revealing all my accomplices.

At last, he said, the court would investigate the matter further and deal most severely with me if more evidence were found incriminating me in this plot.

He then proceeded to question me about other matters. He never reverted to this plot again.

A month later, on October 1 or 2, 1951, an issue of the Jen Min Jih Pao of Peking, the official paper of the Peking communist party, was passed around to the prisoners, as a privilege. In those days no daily paper was issued regularly to us, as later.

A cell-mate, who knew a little English and had read this issue of October 1 or 2, told me he had read about a plot to murder Mao Tse-tung in October, 1950, and that the plot had been discovered in time to prevent it and arrest the conspirators. He added that two foreigners had been shot as conspirators in this plot.

One was Riva, an Italian, and the other was Yamaguchi, a Japanese.

A cold chill went down my back.

Both Riva and Yamaguchi were Catholics whom I knew. Both had devoted wives who were devout Catholics and each had a lovely family of four children. Moreover, shortly before my arrest I had met Mrs. Riva, an American by birth, who told me the police had informed her that Tony, her husband, would be deported in a month or two. This devout Catholic and devoted wife had sold her own excellent library of several hundred volumes for waste paper, but kept her husband's library for his use after his release. The police urged her to leave China but she said she wanted to wait until Tony was deported and leave with him.

Mrs. Yamaguchi I met a week or so before my arrest. I met her in the Peking police office for the foreigners, where she had come to pick up her exit visa. She was a Doctor of Philosophy from the Sorbonne, and spoke excellent French but poor English. In my best French, which was very poor, I inquired about her husband, herself and her family. She later told Mrs. Riva that she was pleased that I had had the courage to speak to her, and even in the police station. She said everybody else avoided her and feared to speak to her.

At the news of the murdering of these two men by the communists, I felt shocked. I also felt extremely sorry for their widows and children.

For three years I did not know whether or not I would be shot because of my refusing to "reform my thinking" to satisfy the government and to a lesser extent because in my sleep, I had allowed myself to be cajoled into a false confession of having been the leader of this "plot" to assassinate Mao Tse-tung.

13

Squatting

"By the Living God, I swear I am not and never was an agent or spy of the American Government," I cried out.

"Ha! ha! He believes in God!"

For days and nights the judge had been pressing me to confess that I was an American agent or spy. He had put me in fetters and hand-cuffs; he had sentenced me to death; he had kept me awake; he had pressed and made himself hoarse shouting and cursing me, to confess I was an American agent. I had stoutly denied I was, or had ever been, an American agent.

At one of these court sessions, I realized that I was in a position in which an oath is allowed by Catholic theology.

"By the Living God, I swear I am not and never was an American agent or spy," I cried out.

At this, the female interpreter, who I was told was an American-born Chinese, threw up her arms and rollicked back and forth in hilarious derision of me.

"Ha! ha!" this blasphemous cadre of the communist government of China laughingly shouted in contempt, "He believes in God!" So spoke a court official of a government that professes freedom of religious belief and forbids ridicule of religion. It is hard for the devil to hide his tail.

This pressing me to confess being an American agent went on for days and nights.

My judge had given me to understand that I would soon be

released if I cleared up my confession. When I told him the truth, he would usually look at a paper before him, evidently to see if my statement agreed with his paper and then look up at me, pound on his desk, and shout, "Liar! Your statement is a lie!"

It became evident to me that his idea of truth differed from mine. To me a statement is true when it agrees with reality. To him it was true when it agreed with the instructions his superiors gave him or, as Tito, the Russian-Serbian chu chang I had, put it so often: "Truth is what the 'people' say it is." And of course the "people" in China are Mao Tse-tung and all who agree with him and support him.

I soon began to think that the communists, even when they talked English, spoke a different language from the English speaking world, including me. "Peace," "democracy," "to help," "liberty," "the people," certainly have one set of meanings in current English and quite another and arbitrary one, when employed by communists.

I came to the conclusion that no prisoner could get anywhere with his communist captors until he spoke the same language as they did.

This conclusion of mine was of course wrong, but it is one a prisoner may easily draw and put into practice, in the face of the bewilderment, helplessness, and confusion in which he eventually finds himself, and the many and prolonged tortures to which he is subjected.

Hence, I began to think in those awful days that I would have to accept the communists' concept of truth.

Add to this the idea I had, that the communists were chiefly concerned in destroying my reputation, one way or the other, to justify their seizure of Fu Jen University.

Prisoner Wang, the merchant, was in contact with my judge and prison officers. He received instructions from them in his assignment to "help" me—that is, force me one way or the other

—to confess I was an American agent. He repeatedly told me that there was a large deportation of prisoners of foreign nationalities scheduled for October 1951, and that if I cleared up my confessions I would surely be among these deportees.

Then one night the judge used a new torture and a new accusation.

He ordered me to squat. The Chinese often squat: the buttocks resting on the heels. This is a position of rest for them. For the average Westerner this position is painful.

I could not squat, partly because I had never done so before, and to begin in my fifty-first year to try to squat, which involved stretching the sinews of my legs that had lost much of their elasticity, was indeed painful. Add to this, the condition of my ankles and legs. Fetters caused much pain to the former while my legs were swollen due to the fetters. Balance was made more difficult with my hands handcuffed behind my back and holding my head erect to look at the face of the cruel judge as I was ordered to do. I also wore old style Chinese shoes which had no heels. If any one who has not acquired the ability to squat from youth thinks this is a painless position, I would advise him to try it at night, in his stocking feet, before retiring. He should also hold his arms behind his back, so the wrists touch, and hold his head erect.

I found this position painful and as time went on, it became more painful. The judge shouted questions at me, pounding the desk with his fist. The interpreter, a male in this session, the recorder, and the guard joined in the tou cheng or shouting accusation.

One night, around this time, I thought for certain I would be literally torn to pieces, dismembered to death.

The cruel judge forced me to squat.

The Sepo guard held me from falling over, by pressing his foot on my back with my hands handcuffed behind my back and my ankles fettered, so that I could hardly breathe. He had pulled hands full of hair out of my head.

Shortly before this when I had refused to squat, the recorder, to force me down into a squat, yanked my ear so that blood streamed through my heavily grown beard. I thought my ear was half torn off and I would be slowly and cruelly killed by dismemberment.

Yet these violent tortures made me more stubborn. I refused to confess what they pressed me to confess. I was prepared to die rather than confess falsely.

·14·

A False Confession

THE JUDGE THEN ordered me to confess my spying activities in the U. S. before coming to China. I maintained I had done no spying in the U. S.

This went on for an hour or so, while I was squatting.

The pain was excruciating.

To gain at least a moment of relief, I fell back on the floor, the dirty floor, stretching out my two legs.

What a relief to stretch out my legs for only a moment! The guard, shouting at me to get up, seized me by my hair and pulled me up.

I stood up. It was a relief to stand up. I was then forced to squat again.

Questioning, shouting by the judge were resumed. After a period of time, I again fell back, sprawling over the floor for a moment's respite. The guard again seized me by the hair, pulling me up to my feet, then forcing me down to a squatting position. The questions continued.

This went on for some hours. I had literally wiped the concrete floor. My clothes, already dirty from weeks of continued wear, became more filthy from the dirt on the floor.

The guard, after a few falls of mine, held me in position by putting his foot on my back and pressing down. This made breathing very difficult.

After hours of this my head was in a whirl.

To relieve myself, I started to tell about my attendance at open air meetings, and two hall meetings of the American

Students Union, a national "progressive" organization at the University of Chicago, where I was a graduated student of geology.

This interested the judge.

He then allowed me to stand up. It was now painful to straighten my knees in order to stand erect, but it was such a relief to stand!

I then went into details about my casual dropping in on these three or four "progressive" student meetings and picking up their hand bills.

This was collecting intelligence according to the judge! Dropping in on meetings opened to all, and to which all were invited was collecting intelligence!

"What did you do with this intelligence?" the judge asked.

"I told it to a friend of mine," I replied.

"He was a government agent, was he not?"

"No," I replied.

"He was!" the judge replied and insisted on it.

"He was not," I answered. "He knew an F.B.I. agent as a friend but was not an agent himself."

"Ah! he knew an F.B.I. agent, and reported to the F.B.I. the intelligence you collected."

"I know nothing about such."

"Can you deny it?"

"I know nothing about such," I repeated.

"Then he did transmit your intelligence to the F.B.I."

In this manner the session ended.

I returned to my cell, full of perspiration, with my clothes dirtier than ever, and my hair all disheveled.

In the next session, I was submitted to the same torture of squatting. The judge insisted that I was an American agent.

At last I thought, the judge and the Chinese government know I am not an American agent, everybody knows this, but the government wants to disgrace me. I am like an actor in a play, taking the part of Julius Caesar. All know I am not really Julius Caesar, but in the play I say I am. Now, all know I am not an American agent but I am pressed to say I am. It would be no lie to say I am such because no one would be deceived.

"I will disgrace myself before the communists by confessing I am an F.B.I. agent. Then after my release, I will send a denial of this from Hong Kong to the government in Peking. If they publish my false confession, I will publish my denial," I thought.

With my mind full of such thoughts and my weakened exhausted body reeking with the pain of fetters and hand cuffs, I confessed falsely.

"I am an F.B.I. agent," I said.

I was immediately allowed to stand up, amidst the cats and dogs I saw running around the court room. It was weakness on my part to make such a false confession. I do not defend it.

When I returned to my cell, I felt thoroughly miserable. Never had I experienced such a feeling of guilt, of confirmed weakness. "I, a priest, a rector of the Fu Jen Catholic University, making a false confession, and such a confession: that I was a spy, an agent of the American government, an F.B.I. man. I have disgraced myself, my religious community, Fu Jen University, my Church! What will the Catholics of Fu Jen now think of me? Will this scandalize them that they will weaken in their faith? Heaven knows these good Chinese Catholics need encouragement, a good example. I, who formerly exhorted them to be steadfast, have fallen!"

The mental anguish, mental torture was great. Day and night I reproached myself, but I hoped well-meaning people outside would understand.

·15·

A Denial and a Retraction

MY FIRST repudiation of my false F.B.I. confession was made shortly after the confession had been made.

No surcease or lessening of my tortures, which I had expected, followed my false confession of being an F.B.I agent. On the contrary they continued. The judge seemed more vicious than ever. He told my chu chang that I had only begun to confess and he intended to torture me throughout the coming night, from sunset to after sunrise, by making me squat ten or twelve hours, unless I confessed fully as he wanted.

The forces of nature intervened, however. I had suffered so much from the tortures so far inflicted that I found myself sick, shaking with chills. The elderly Manchu physician noticed this and reported it to the chu chang who sent me to the prison physician. I told him how I felt. I added that I had often had malaria during my six years in tropical Africa and that I felt like I had another attack of this fever. He took my temperature and gave me powders that served as a panacea since he gave them for practically all ailments. This physician, however, impressed me as a kind man—the only openly kind man in the prison—although he appeared to me to be more ready to lecture his patients to confess and reform than he was to give them medical advice.

This kind physician, however, reported to the prison authorities that I was a sick man and should be allowed a night's rest.

I was given my first night's rest!

When I was called to court again, the judge wanted to know my number as an F.B.I. agent. I was unprepared for this and spent a hectic night denying I had a number. The next day I decided I had to give a number and selected one that could easily be remembered, otherwise I would be giving a different one every day. So I decided on a number of four digits, the first two of which were multiplied by two to equal the second two as 3264 or 3162. I forget which one was used. I submitted this as my F.B.I. number.

Then I was asked what letter preceded my number. I remembered that my serial number in the army was preceded by "O" to signify "officer." So I said my F.B.I. number was preceded by "I" to signify "Inspector."

So the sad comedy went on. I had placed my head in the noose, which was drawn tighter and tighter.

"When did you join the F.B.I.?"

"Where did you join the F.B.I.?"

"Who recommended you?"

"Who was your chief or superior officer?"

"What was your rank?"

"What identification did you have?"

These and more questions were hurled at me night after night. Each came unexpected. Each was struggled with. Each was eventually answered. I became more and more wretched.

The mental suffering became more and more intense.

Then one day, I resolved to straighten matters out, to repudiate my false confessions.

That night when my court session opened, I told the judge I had a statement I wanted to make. He ordered me to make it.

"I am not an F.B.I. agent. I never was an F.B.I. agent. My confession that I was one was false and I wish to correct it!"

Then the judge sat back and rather quietly in a rather fatherly manner asked about my family, about each member, taking one by one, inquiring about his or her name, occupation, habit, when I last saw him or her, etc., centering my mind on those I loved best. He was telling me in so many words: "Have you forgotten your family? Don't you want to see them again? The way you are going, you will never see them—you are simply leading yourself into a lot of torture that will be terminated by your execution."

I stood this for the entire night, without retracting my denial or acknowledging my false confession.

But the next day prisoner Wang and prisoner Lu started working on me. Prisoner Wang was a merchant who spoke English. Prisoner Lu had been a colonel in the secret service of the Chinese Nationalist Army. He had become very "progressive" and communistic in his thinking. Both were in cells different from mine but they were daily sent into my cell to take over and direct the "helping," that is, pressing, torturing, and the tou chenging of me to force a confession out of me.

Lu was the chief. Wang was usually interpreter for Lu who spoke little English but they often conferred about how to treat me, or they would take turns working on me.

Now Wang took matters mostly into his own hands and began to lecture me.

"Well, Rigney, how was the court session last night?" he began in the usual fashion of a chu cheng, asking a prisoner all about the previous court session, about which he had, in this case, been thoroughly informed by the judge.

I told him I had denied my confession of being an F.B.I. agent.

"What!" he shrieked.

"You denied your confession! My God! Rigney, what have you done? I thought you had more sense than that! Here, everything was going on so well! You had confessed well; you were almost finished with your confession. A little more and you would have been finished. You would then have been allowed to sleep as you need to. You would then have been allowed a hot bath. What is more, you would soon be deported.

The government does not want to try to re-educate you. You are a foreigner and too old anyway for re-education. All the government wants of you is a confession and then let you go. But you have spoilt everything. You will never be deported now. You will be shot in a few days. What is the good of such fool-heartedness? Washington cannot help you. Wall Street has long ago forgotten you. Do you think the U. S. government will erect a monument to you? — — —." And so he went on and on and on and on, hour after hour.

It was most unbearable. I had to listen with every mark of attention. When I showed signs of fatigue, I was obliged to stand up and later kneel for more hours. This continued all day.

As far as I can remember, my regular judge did not preside in my court session that night but the interpreter or recorder took his place and questioned me about matters not pertaining to my F.B.I. confession.

The next day Wang continued with his tongue lashing, until after some hours I felt I could stand it no longer. "The time is not ripe for denying my false confession," I thought. So, truly weary and exhausted in mind and body, I said, "Yes, I am an F.B.I. agent."

At this Wang and Lu were elated. They had won.

They advised me to report the acknowledgment of my F.B.I. confession to the judge at the next night session. I had at the last moment gotten some sense, they told me, and had saved my life.

In the next court session, I told the judge that I had received some "help" from my cell-mates and as a consequence wanted to retract the denial of my F.B.I. confession—that I acknowledged my confession—I was an F.B.I. man.

He very graciously forgave me the great "crime" I had committed. I would not be punished for such a "crime" but it should not happen again. Another such mistake would be fatal. He then spent the night giving me a long lecture on government policy and government leniency to prisoners who confessed and reformed. He even granted me the privilege of sitting down in the court session.

For the next few days, he dealt less harshly with me. It was evident that he was straining himself to make the impression of being "kind" to me. Perhaps he thought that the previous cruel treatment had been carried too far and brought poor results. A show of "kindness" might bring better results.

But I soon felt more wretched than ever. My mental agony was worse than before. Here, a couple of weeks previously, I had been ready to die for the truth. Since then, I had made a false confession, retracted it, gone through a couple of days and nights of acute struggle and suffering in resisting efforts to force me to retract this denial, but had weakened again and retracted it. I was back and deeper in the hole.

·16·

Praying

"RIGNEY, what are you doing?" shouted chu chang Lu one morning in December 1951, as he saw me squatting and praying, waiting to be allowed to file out to the open latrines.

"I am just squatting waiting for the officer to open the door for us," I replied.

Daily my judge subjected me to the torture of squatting. Hours each day I suffered from this but began to notice that squatting was becoming less painful. To harden myself, I began to squat in my cell whenever I could.

On this particular morning my chu chang interpreted my squatting as a position of prayer. Although I was praying, my squatting position had nothing to do with my devotions.

"Rigney, do you ever pray?" Lu then asked.

"Yes, I pray."

There was silence.

I had answered Lu's question and was satisfied to let matters stand.

Lu evidently made a mental note of my statement, since he later reported to the prison officer that I prayed on many occasions and even counted my prayers on my fingers. This was true when I prayed my rosary, using my fingers to count instead of beads.

"Rigney, are you praying?" roared chu chang Lu, on a cold, bleak day in January 1952, as I sat motionless, excepting for the slight movement of my lips in prayer which I thought could not be noticed.

"Yes, I am praying."

"Praying! What are you praying for? You should be thinking about your crimes," bellowed this ex-army colonel and one time anti-communist.

"God cannot help you," he continued in his blasphemy, "Only the 'people's' government can help you. You fool, you are wasting your time with your silly prayers!

"Stop praying!

"Do not pray anymore!

"Think of the crimes you have committed against the Chinese 'people'!"

But I continued to pray. Everyday, I prayed from three to ten rosaries for my daily office and other intentions, and many more prayers. Meditation became sweet as never before.

The wicked communists could deprive me of my liberty, torture me and set their running dogs among my cell-mates to join with them, in torturing me day after day for over four years, but they could not abolish the Omnipresence of the Most Blessed Trinity. They could not prevent me from turning my mind and raising my heart above the foulness of their world, to Divine Realities.

"Do you ever pray, Rigney?" asked the officer one day in the spring of 1953.

"Yes."

"Pu hsing! Pu hsing! (That is not allowed! That is not allowed!)" this huge, brutal type of a communist prison official said, his face distorted with anger.

"How often do you pray?" he continued.

"I pray every day."

"Pu hsing! pu hsing!" he shouted as he shook his fist in my face, and lectured me that it was forbidden to pray, at any time, even while in bed, before sleeping or on awakening in the morning.

And so this official of a regime, the communist regime of

China which asserts that religions are free, that the Church has no ground to complain, went on curtain lecturing me, threatening me, forbidding me to pray.

On the same day, after the official had left the cell, prisoner Julian, a "Catholic" Eurasian of foreign nationality, took up the theme where the officer had left off, and attempted to persuade me to stop praying.

I had been arrested under the fictitious charge of being a spy. Now, I thought, if the communist government punishes me, by shooting me, or sentencing me to a prison term because I prayed, they would be clarifying my case, removing the smoke screen of hypocrisy they had emitted around it. They would make my case an undoubtedly religious case.

So, I stood my ground.

Julian, I knew, had been delegated to "help" me, to watch my every move, to listen to my every word, and report all to the government. He spoke English well and was allowed to talk to me in that language.

"Why do you pray, Rigney?" Julian said.

"I pray because I am obliged to pray."

Julian then embarked on an effort to convince me to give up praying!

However, this young opportunist of little character and less principle, met with no success.

I refused to repudiate my habit of prayer.

To the last day, in prison, I prayed and meditated. I often pitied my pagan, non-Christian cell-mates who did not find the consolation I did, in prayer.

In the fall of 1953, Han, an English-speaking Chinese had been appointed by the prison authorities to "help" me. He was allowed to talk to me in English.

Han watched me so closely that one night he noticed my lips moving as if in prayer. The next morning he asked me to explain why my lips were moving the previous night while I slept.

The explanation seemed simple to me, but I preferred to keep it to myself. I usually went to sleep praying. Consequently, it should not surprise one if my lips continued to move in sleep.

"A sleeping man is not responsible for his actions," I told Han.

After this, Han often told me that on the previous night he had noticed my lips moving, while I slept, as if I were praying.

On Christmas day, 1953, Han told me he had gotten up many many times during the night to see if my lips were moving as in prayer. He also wanted to know if I had arisen during the night to perform some secret religious Christmas rite.

Often, when I counted something as the days on my fingers, the chu chang at the time or some activist assigned to "help" would ask me if I were counting prayers on my fingers.

How I longed to celebrate the Holy Sacrifice of the Mass!
How I longed to pray my divine office!
How I longed to receive the Holy Eucharist!
How I longed to visit and pray before the Blessed Sacrament!

All these were denied me for the four years and two months, or to be more exact, for the one thousand five hundred and nine days I was in the communist prisons of Peking, China.

Often I dreamed of celebrating the Holy Sacrifice of the Mass, usually in the University chapel of the Divine Word or in the immaculately clean and beautifully decorated chapel of those good Sisters of Fu Jen, the Holy Ghost Missionary Sisters.

Those were happy dreams. They came to an abrupt and

painful end when I awoke to find where I was: in prison, a communist prison, modeled after hell.

In the winter of 1953, prisoner Luke, the foreign physician and a Catholic, fell into a short conversation with me on church architecture, at a time when we were alone in the cell. Luke was a gifted, versatile man with ideas about church architecture for China that pleased me. He drew a rough ground plan of a church in the form of a Latin cross.

Some days later, chu chang Tito saw this drawing. On learning from Luke that it had been sketched for me, he shouted, "Rigney asked you to do this? Look, that is done in the shape of a cross! He asked you to do this, Luke, you stupid ass, to fool you! He is using religion to gain your sympathy, to keep you from reforming!" Turning to me he roared, "Rigney, you will answer for this crime, in due time!"

"Ts'ao Lan Tzu is like hell," I often thought.

In Ts'ao Lan Tzu, no one was allowed to pray.

No one was allowed to conduct or lead Church services.

No one was allowed or given the opportunity to attend Church services.

No one was allowed to administer the sacraments.

No one was allowed to receive the sacraments.

No one was allowed to think of God.

No one was allowed to talk about any subject even remotely connected with religion.

It was strictly forbidden to be friendly with any one. It was forbidden to show sympathy to a prisoner suffering of handcuffs or fetters.

It was not only allowed but even encouraged to hate other prisoners.

It was allowed and encouraged to persecute, torture other prisoners.

Prisoners were subjected to various kinds of physical and mental tortures.

"Hell is like this!" I thought.

But the one consolation was that Ts'ao Lan Tzu would not last forever. It would come to an end some day. I would be shot, die in prison from a disease or torture, or I would be released. The end would eventually come. It might take a long time coming, but it would come.

Hell on the other hand is eternal, endless.

I learned one big lesson, in Ts'ao Lan Tzu—I must save my soul.

I knew this necessity before, but here it was brought home to me as never before.

The hell of the temporal Ts'ao Lan Tzu is bad enough! With God's help, I will avoid the eternal Ts'ao Lan Tzu—the eternal hell!

In this hell of Ts'ao Lan Tzu, no one laughed—a real, hearty laugh. Some prisoners indulged in mock laughter; derision over another prisoner's mistakes; forced expressions of false delight in reported communist victories, etc., but no one ever really, truly laughed.

Before my arrest, I was quite gay. I had a sense of humor and was quick to joke and laugh. I was such even during the 20 months when the clouds of my impending arrest hung over me.

But now in communist prisons, I never laughed. I never was gay or merry.

I felt that I had changed, lost something, that I could never be my old self again.

It seemed I was damaged mentally, psychologically wounded, and the spiritual scars of these wounds of my mental suffering of four years and two months would forever remain.

·17·

More Denials and the Cold

I HAD GONE through the anguish of denying my false confession and had lost this regained ground by retraction of my denial. I was worse off than before.

It is difficult to remember the sequences of events of the early days of my imprisonment. But I recall that a few days after my retraction of my first denial of my false confession, I found myself in great mental anguish. Finally I decided to deny my false confession by a written statement. Wang and Lu exploded in anger when I told them I wanted paper on which to write this denial. Lu soon arranged with the guard to allow him to leave the cell, evidently to report my plans to the prison authorities.

On Lu's return to the cell, he and Wang warned me that to sign a written denial of my confession would result in my execution.

"The government has evidence that you are an F.B.I. man. If you admit this, you would help yourself. If you deny it by a written statement, you will be shot in a few days," Wang said.

I struggled with myself: "The government claims they have evidence that I am an F.B.I. agent. The awful aspect of this is that the government alone, whom I do not trust, will judge the validity of this evidence. I will have nothing to say about it. I will not be informed of it. I will never be allowed to refute it. I will never be allowed a competent, reliable counsel to defend me when this evidence shall be reviewed. The evidence must be some flimsy piece of a distorted, exaggerated account of me. If I sign a written denial, I will surely be shot in a few days. But better be shot than live in a falsehood. God knows the truth, that I am not an F.B.I. agent. If I am shot, the communists will shoot me under the false charges of being an American spy, who had his just desert meted out to him, but the Good God will know I am innocent and am dying for the truth."

Wang lectured me all day.

In the late afternoon, I wrote out my denial. Wang and Lu were upset and advised me to think the matter over before signing the statement. I delayed signing about an hour, then signed and handed it in.

I was certain I would be shot in a few days. I remember I tore a sheet of shou chih (a low grade of paper such as I have never seen in the U. S.) into about 48 pieces, each about 2½ inches by 3½, for toilet use. As I was tearing up this paper, I thought, "Why prepare so many pieces of shou chih; I will be shot in three or four days."

On the following day, Wang and Lu began lecturing me again. They told me I had made a big mistake, etc. This went on for how long I do not remember, until I could stand it no longer and I retracted. Again I was thrown into deep dejection and anguish.

So I denied my false confession and retracted my denial some five times. Each time after the denial, I was subjected to a long tongue-lashing from Wang—until I could stand it no longer and decided the time was not ripe for my denial and retracted.

Around the end of August, the judge demanded that I confess my connections with German Nazi espionage agencies. I told him I had no such connections and knew nothing about any German Nazi espionage group. He shouted, pounded his desk, called me a liar, a guttersnipe—threatened to shoot me, etc.

He made me squat for hours. Once he stopped questioning me, leaving me in the agony of squatting. After a half hour or so, he looked up from the work on his desk that had engaged his attention and sneered saying, "Now pray to Mary. See if she can help you!"

As a matter of fact, I had been praying for strength to bear up under my ordeal. After this blasphemy, I prayed God to note his mockery against His Mother, to confound this blasphemer, and by showing His power in His own way, deliver me.

In the middle or late part of September, my night and early morning court session ceased. What a relief! How grand it was to sleep the entire night through. Each morning, on awakening, I fervently thanked the Holy Triune God for the night's rest I had just enjoyed.

"I am cold," I said as I shuddered in the evenings of late September, but no relief was offered me until sometime in October when a light cotton Japanese Army summer jacket was given me.

This was a relief for a week or so. It grew chillier in October and I suffered from the cold. I asked for a second jacket. Lu brought one in and told me I could have it as soon as I cleared up my confession.

Day after day, he came into my cell, carrying this extra jacket, keeping it in my view, while I shuddered from the cold, and offered it to me if I would clear up my confession.

I suffered much from the cold. There was no heat. The window was kept open. Cold was now added to hunger, the pains of fetters, the mental anguish of living a falsehood, and the other ordinary inconveniences of a wretched, damp, rat-infested cell.

At last I was given a mien au or cotton padded jacket. For a week or so this was enough, except for my feet that never were warm until at night I wrapped myself in the mien pei or cotton blanket which the prison had issued to me in late October. It was badly in need of washing since it gave off an unpleasant odor of the feet of the one or more prisoners who had previously used it.

Soon the mien au was insufficient to keep me warm. I sat all day on the wooden kang, shivering, my breath steamed in the cold. My feet soon were covered with 18 or 20 cold sores. I had only summer pants on. I was then wearing the heaviest fetters, weighing almost twenty pounds. When I wrapped myself in the smelly mien pei or cotton blanket, my feet on getting warm pained me for half an hour or so.

Sometime in 1950, I was asked by a reliable and good friend if I had a way of relaying a message from Chairman Mao Tse-tung to President Truman.

This question shocked me. Had my friend unknowingly been led to ask me a trap question? I had never had at my disposal or employed other than ordinary legitimate means of communication or correspondence: the mail, telegraph, cable or telephone.

"I have no special means of communication," I said. "The only means I have are the ordinary ones as the mail, telegraph, cable and telephone.

"If President Mao wants me to deliver a message for him to President Truman, I could only use these ordinary, legitimate means. I could take a message, but in that case Chairman Mao Tse-tung would have to provide me with the exit permit to leave China, which I have been waiting months for, and give me his message personally. I would then deliver this to President Truman, in person."

The other person continued: "Mao Tse-tung would like to form a coalition government with Fu Tso-I and Chiang Kai-

Shek that would be pro-American rather than pro-Russian. He would like to inform President Truman of this, in a way the pro-Russian section of the Chinese Communist Party would be unable to learn about."

This seemed rather unusual. I certainly did not want to be involved in sectional strifes within the party, if the matter were true.

I was approached again with the same request which I answered in the same way.

At least five others knew the contents of this request and that it had been made to me.

Later, three of these five were in Ts'ao Lan Tzu prison with me. None of them wore chains, as stubborn prisoners, and I was told two were so far advanced in their re-education that they were removed to the reformatory where special privileges were enjoyed. These three had evidently confessed well, including about this Mao-Fu-Chiang coalition and the Mao-Truman message.

For a long time I refused to mention anything about this message and the part I had been requested to play in delivering it.

At last, I concluded the government must know all about it from these fellow prisoners or from others not in Ts'ao Lan Tzu and I was only asking for torture, trying to hide what the government knew.

So one day in the Autumn of 1952, I told the judge about the matter of the proposed coalition, as well as the message and the stand I had taken.

The next day, to my astonishment and relief, the judge brought up the matter and said: "This is all pure rubbish! Forget all about it! Do not mention it again!"

Yes, linking Mao Tse-tung with Chiang Kai-Shek and President Truman was not to be heard of and the matter was not to be touched.

The alternative could be that the original question with

its explanation about a coalition, pro-American government was a bait, a test to discover whether I employed illegitimate means of communications as a secret radio, or was promoting the formation of a new pro-American government in China.

·18·

Handcuffs and Fetters

THE FETTERS I wore cut deep into my ankles. My leather lowcut shoes were ruined by then. For a day or so I protected my ankles by wrapping my pants around my ankles under the fetters. These pants were strong U. S. army pants, which I had worn in the army during the Second World War. The fetters cut through this tough cloth, stained with my blood. When the judge saw this protection of my ankles, he ordered me to remove my pants from beneath the fetters and keep them removed. My bare ankles must not be protected from the rusty, rough, dirty, iron fetters.

My feet and legs swelled up. My feet swelled so much it was impossible to put on my shoes. There was a discarded pair of old worn-out Chinese cloth shoes in the cell. The chu chang gave me these to wear but they soon fell to pieces, and I went to court in my bare feet.

My arms and hands swelled up from the handcuffs.

These fetters and handcuffs became painful.

From them I learned the meaning of "wretchedness."

Seven times I was handcuffed with my hands behind my back for times ranging from one day to seven days and nights. The first time was a few days after my arrest. I forget the reason the judge gave when he ordered them on.

I ask the reader to use his or her imagination, in judging and understanding the torture of having your hands handcuffed behind your back. Aside from the pain of the rough, dirty, rusty iron cutting into your skin and flesh, every time you move your hand, there are other sufferings: humiliations, insults you undergo too delicate to write or talk about. This is especially regarding acts associated with urination and bowel movements.

You cannot bathe yourself. You cannot wash your face. You cannot comb your hair if you have long hair. You cannot scratch yourself when the lice bite.

If you wear spectacles, who cleans them of the sweat, dust, and grease that collects on them?

It is most difficult to sleep, on the hard wooden kang. You lie on one arm. This is painful. Every position you take, lying down, is painful.

How can you eat?

The first time I was handcuffed, the chu chang ordered a cell-mate to feed me. Later I had to eat unaided the best I could, like a dog. My wo tou was thrown on the kang with curses, then placed above the stinking urine bucket by Lu, the chu chang, and I was obliged to kneel at the side of the kang, over this stinking urine bucket which was under the kang, and eat my wretched wo tou, like a dog.

Creatures, cell-mates who claimed to be human beings, subjected me to these indignities. Chu chang Lu, the ex-Kuomintang colonel, was the leader in all this, in his efforts to carry out the orders of his new communist masters who also claimed to be human beings—but perhaps I am wrong, misjudging the Chinese communists. There are no human beings according to marxist communists. A human being is a spiritual animal, but marxist communists deny spirituality to men. Therefore, they deny that we are human. We are only two-legged, upright walking brutes.

We do not have souls.

We do not have spirituality.

We are not human!

The idea of being "human" is just so much bourgeois, imperialistic, religious rubbish, according to the prophet Karl Marx.

The last time I was handcuffed was in punishment for refusing to accuse Father Joseph Meiners, S.V.D., and Professor Dr. William Bruell, of being Gestapos. The former had been on the staff of Fu Jen University and had manifested much zeal in developing the Legion of Mary at Fu Jen. The latter was an efficient teacher of chemistry, who had remained at his post as head of the Department of Chemistry of Fu Jen University, until the communists forced him out. When the judge accused Father Meiners to me of being a member of the Gestapo and asked me what evidence I knew to substantiate this, I said, "I know of no fact to indicate or prove that Father Joseph Meiners is a Gestapo, and personally I do not believe he is one."

At this, the judge blew up into a rage of fury, shouting, pounding his desk, cursing me, calling me a liar and the like.

I held my ground, in spite of all the abuse dealt out to me.

Then the judge accused Professor Bruell the same as he had Father Meiners, and I replied in a similar manner.

Again the judge fell into a tantrum.

This went on over Father Meiners and Professor Bruell for some 3 or 4 hours throughout the morning session.

I was then handcuffed with my hands behind my back.

The heaviest fetters had already been placed on me. These weighed around twenty pounds.

It was so difficult to try to sleep lying down that I sat up.

The nights were cold and my blanket was wrapped around me but every night it soon unloosened, and I became very cold.

For seven days and nights, I wore these handcuffs. My wrists and arms were very much swollen.

When these handcuffs were removed, as usual it was very painful to bring my arms around to their normal position, or in front of me. Especially it was difficult to lift them up. It took two or three days of practice to lift them above my head.

For several months my wrists were numb.

Men, prelates, priests, brothers and women—yes, nuns, the most sensitive of creatures, underwent these unspeakable indignities!

Then there were the fetters.

The pain of these instruments of torture became more intense day by day. Each step was agony as the horrible, heavy, rough iron ground back and forth into my flesh.

I would have preferred being shot to walking fifty feet in fetters.

And the sadistic judge called me back and forth, three, four or five times a day to his hellish court which was about 300 feet away.

I got blood poison from these filthy fetters and would have died, but the communists wanted me to live. I was of more value to them alive than dead. A living prisoner can confess. A dead one cannot.

So my fetters were removed this time and some two dozen penicillin injections or what was told me was penicillin were administered to me.

It is easy for the communists to kill a prisoner without the formality of shooting him. Fetters, exposure to cold, starvation, are some of the means at their disposal to do away with prisoners.

I remember one night while slowly making my way to the court in the excruciating pain of these fetters, with a cruel Sepo guard at my rear, cursing and shouting at me to move faster. In utter abandonment I prayed the only prayer I could think of and utter: the words of Our Blessed Lord on the cross, words I began to understand for the first time! "My God, My God, why hast Thou forsaken me?" Matthew, XXVII, 46.

·19·

Divine Word Missionaries,
Food and Clothing

"Who were the F.B.I. spies in the Divine Word Society in the U.S.A.?" asked the judge in a court session, one day in November.

I loved the Divine Word Mission Society to which I belong, but I never realized how much I loved it until the communists calumniated it, accused it of being a spying organization.

The Divine Word Mission Society, a spying organization? Outrageous!

The court asked me to write the history of the Divine Word Mission Society. I did this, describing how a pious, German priest, the Venerable Father Arnold Janssen founded this society in 1875, to train foreign missionaries and conduct foreign missions. The court was very angry because I did not write that Father Arnold Janssen was a spy who founded a big espionage organization which he called the Divine Word Society. The judge also claimed that St. Mary's Mission Seminary, Techny, Illinois, U.S.A., was a spy training center.

St. Mary's Mission Seminary, a spy training center? Outrageous! I had studied there eleven of the fourteen years I spent preparing for the priesthood and loved this beautiful spot very much. I had been ordained a priest there. Now the communists maintained that it was a training center for spies!

Such utter rubbish!

The court, however, continued pressing me to confess what members of the American Provinces of the Divine Word Missionaries were F.B.I. agents. Then one night after retiring time, when all the cell-mates were in bed, Lu was called out of the cell. I had been transferred to Lu's cell, where he was chu chang. Wang was also in this cell.

In a few minutes Lu returned and ordered Wang and me to get up. He then told me through Wang as interpreter that he had just been called out by my judge who had instructed him to press me to name the American Divine Word Missionaries who were F.B.I. men. The judge further stated that there would be no sleep for any one in my cell this or the following nights until I confessed.

So there I was, sitting up shivering in the cold of a November's night in Peking, keeping the rest of my cell-mates awake.

I told Wang and Lu that I knew of no American Divine Word Missionary who was an F.B.I agent. They insisted that there were many. We carried on like this for one or two hours. Then, I considered, for me to keep all my cell-mates awake night after night was no small matter. So I said I knew some American Divine Word Missionaries who were F.B.I. men and after about an hour, listed some members of the Divine Word Missionaries outside of China, out of range of the Chinese communists.

With this we were all allowed to sleep.

Furthermore, my fetters were removed and I was allowed my first hot bath in four months.

What a relief it was to have those heavy fetters removed! My ankles were sore and full of wounds from these and especially from the first pair of medium sized fetters that had cut into my skin and flesh. It was three months before my ankles healed, because walking kept the wounds open. The bath was another great relief for which I had longed, for many months.

Our cell and another cell were led to the bath house. We entered a room about 10 feet by 12 feet where we undressed, piling our clothes on the floor. Each prisoner laid his clothes together, hoping to recover them with little trouble. We then passed into the bath room which was about 20 feet square with two pools each about 8 feet square. Each pool was filled with hot water that had been often used by the cadres and guards of the prison as well as by prisoners of other cells.

We sat in the hot water, then rubbed ourselves with a wet towel. It was forbidden to use soap in the pool and there was no time for every one to soap and rinse outside the pool. Hence, most were satisfied with a soaking and rubbing with hot water alone.

Following this we hastened into the room where our clothes were and as quickly as possible found our clothes, dressed and stood in line outside the bath house to be led back to the cell where most prisoners loudly praised the "good" government for providing an excellent hot bath for us "criminals, enemies of the people."

Such adulation was nauseating to me. It was indulged in on all possible occasions by most prisoners.

I remember one chap in this same cell, a certain Wu, who went one better than the rest in his servile flattery of the government that had ruthlessly thrown him and millions of others into prison. Every morning on hearing the signal to rise, he would immediately, before getting out of his bed-roll, break out singing a communist song as loudly as he could to draw the attention of guards and officers.

I felt refreshed after this hot bath.

Moreover, I was issued and allowed to put on mien ku or cotton padded pants. I was quite warm now with cotton padded jacket and pants.

But by the end of November, these were not enough to keep me warm. I shivered in the unheated, damp cells from the lack of underwear, heavy winter underwear.

Around the beginning of December, the court allowed me

to buy food after my writing a request for it. I purchased about 16 U.S. dollars worth of food, including meat, apples, eggs, butter (I ordered one pound of butter but was given oleomargarine for which I paid about two U.S. dollars), peanuts, etc. This food with its proteins and fats was greatly needed by me and equally relished.

The court, however, was quite dramatic in delivering it. The judge called me to court, and showed me this food. My eyes almost popped out of their sockets. The food looked so good.

I thanked the judge for it.

Wang went into an ecstasy in his praise of the government. He said he almost cried. He was so moved when the communist government allowed me, an imperialist spy, a great enemy of the Chinese people, to purchase this food. He could not understand how I could be so cold and unmoved after having committed such "crimes" against the "people."

As the days passed, I suffered more and more from the cold. The court staged Act II in trying to win me by "generosity." In the middle of December, the judge informed me that the court would send soldiers to my living quarters at Fu Jen to gather some of my warm clothing and bedding. I was to request these and submit a list of what I wanted, which I did.

Then on Christmas eve, I was called to court where I saw my clothes and bedding in the court room. The judge then wished me a Merry Christmas and released these belongings to me. I thanked him for them but felt that he was unnecessarily dramatic about the whole matter.

Among the clothes I received was a suit of woolen underwear, and a woolen shirt, which I immediately put on. I was then warm. In the early part of January, stoves were set up in the corridors and fires started in them. These, with the heavy clothing, kept me warm for the rest of the winter of 1952.

The fifth denial of my false F.B.I. confession and retraction of this denial occurred, as far as I can remember, in January 1952. The judge was very angry.

"I forbid you to deny this confession again," he said. "If you dare to deny it again, you shall be shot. This is definite! Do you understand?"

"Yes."

Then after about an hour of shouting and cursing me, all the while pounding on the desk like a maniac, he shouted, ordering me to write and sign a statement that I would never again deny my F.B.I. confession and if I did, I would submit to the severest punishment, which meant execution.

I hesitated to do such, that is, to bind myself never to tell the truth about this false confession, never, even under pain of execution.

With my hesitation, the judge grew frantic. The interpreter and recorder joined in shouting at me and demanding this signed statement. True to form the armed guard took his cue from the enraged judge, and joined in the shouting. As I still hesitated, he arose from his seat, took his big pistol by the barrel, raising it high in the air in a gesture of striking, and stepped forward to beat me over the head with the butt or handle of this weapon.

In the midst of this madhouse, I thought, "The time will inevitably come when I will make a final and definite denial of this false confession. The court will then be angry with me for having made a false confession. If I sign the statement these court officials are now demanding, I will have a written document to stand as an excuse for my failure for correcting, at an earlier date, this false confession. Therefore I will write and sign the demanded statement. There can be no doubt that it is extorted from me under pressure, and consequently the court can have no complaint against me, for delaying to correct this false confession."

"I will write and sign such a statement," I said.

The judge then dictated the statement which was to stand as my own free statement, and I signed it.

I was then in the position of being forbidden to tell the truth, forbidden by a communist military court, and had even promised under pain of death not to tell the truth.

In the days and weeks that followed, my mental anguish over this was great, until I resolved at all costs, even life itself, to disregard this written pledge and to repudiate my false confession.

·20·

Moving to the South Compound

"Tou PAO hao ni men ti tung hsi, (All of you pack up your belongings)" the officer said, on January 11, 1952, then closed the cell door.

In a moment the cell was in a state of apparent confusion. Every one was busy throwing together his meager belongings —his bed-roll, bundle of change of clothing used as a pillow, drinking cup, tooth brush, wash pan, soap, towel, pencil, shou chih (toilet paper), salt, chop sticks, bowl and other non-descript items as note books, string on which to hang towels, cell-made playing cards. Not every cell-mate possessed all the above. A newly arrested prisoner or one denied the privilege to write his family, usually had only a bowl and chop sticks.

After a few minutes, the officer returned and called out my name, then the name of another cell-mate, who said he had been a communist and had left the party around 1945, after having belonged to it for 15 years. We were then led across the compound to the southern section, and to cell No. 5.

This cell was an improvement over the three cells I had previously occupied, in the northern section. The others had the bare ground as the floor, and were rat infested. The new cell, however, had a concrete floor. The rest of the cell was the same as the others I had been in.

I spent about fourteen weeks in this and a nearby cell, in both of which Lang was chu chang. They were a bitter fourteen weeks that ended around May 1, 1952.

One cell-mate, a Japanese, spoke very little English, about as much English as I did Chinese. The rest knew no English.

On the very first day in this cell, I was ordered to join the rest of the cell mates as they gathered, sitting in a circle with their legs crossed. Then the study class, a period of indoctrination or brain-washing, began. A newspaper article was read. A review and discussion of it followed.

When it came my turn to talk or recite, I said:

"Wo pu chih tao Chung Kuo-hua. Wo pu ming pei pao. (I do not understand Chinese. I do not understand the newspaper.)"

After questioning me a little further, Lang left me alone.

My inability to speak and understand Chinese well was an asset, as far as the study or brainwashing classes were concerned. It spared me from joining in many discussions in which the Catholic Church or the U.S.A., both of which I loved very much, were grossly misrepresented, calumniated and soundly cursed.

This ineptness in Chinese, on the other hand, was a great drawback for me outside these classes, as in ordinary daily intercourse with cell-mates, including the free time when conversation was allowed. The conversation was limited in scope. We were often told it should be confined to the field of the "people's" China, socialism, communism, marxism, and the like. The manifestation of friendliness, the discussion of questions about one's past life, or former occupied cells or former cell-mates, and of course religion and religious topics, were all taboo.

But in spite of the restricted nature of the conversation, the mere exchange of ideas was a relief.

I was isolated, ordered to sit in a corner, in and out of class. The mental relief of conversation was denied me. This was another torture to which I was subjected.

It was not a severe one in itself. Most of the tortures I suffered were not severe, but the accumulation of these rather mild tortures over a long space of time constituted severe tortures.

In this time, I frequently stated my desire to learn to speak and write Chinese.

It was evident that the communist authorities did not want me to learn Chinese. I repeatedly asked for a suitable book in English for the study of this language. There were many such books. And I had a good one in my room for which I asked when the court sent soldiers to my living quarters to pick up clothing, bedding and the like for me. But this Chinese book was not brought me. I asked to purchase such a book, with no results. I was never told I could not have such a book. The desire was allowed to live on, but its satisfaction was steadfastly denied me. The communists are experts in torturing you, by allowing you to crave for something but denying you satisfaction. How often did I experience this! The more one begs for something, the less likely he will ever get it. The result of this application of animal psychology is that you just cease desiring anything. After all, poverty, low standards of living are quite common in communist China, in spite of all the boasting of great increases in real wages, great raising of living standards, as never before! Hence, the Chinese must be trained, I will not say taught, to desire little or nothing.

Besides refusing me then and to the end of my imprisonment, a suitable book from which to study Chinese, cell-mates in cell 5 were forbidden to explain even in Chinese the meaning of words that I heard in the classes or in ordinary conversation.

A year later, in February 1954, I was allowed to buy a small book about 3 inches by 5 inches in which were some 2370 characters with phonetics alongside them. There were no meanings in English. This book was useful to one who spoke Chinese and wanted to learn characters.

In my case it was a mockery. I felt I was being tantalized.

Anyway I did study Chinese with this book, learning 1500 characters practically all of which I soon forgot when I was unable to continue to study by reason of being ordered to sit in on the classes and other indoctrination nonsense.

·21·

Priests Forever

In the winter of 1952, in cell 6 of the North or B Compound, I discovered that one of the Chinese cell-mates, prisoner Lee, was a Catholic priest. Lee and I were allowed to converse together a little in Latin. However, by agreement, we spoke together only when necessary or in urgent cases. We followed this policy for our own protection. Since we were both priests, talking together often and over long periods would only invite punishment. Father Lee, however, often interpreted for me in the cell, using Latin.

I wanted to receive the sacrament of penance, to go to confession. I had not made a confession since July 1951. No religious ministrations were allowed in this prison. So I bided my time, waiting for an opportunity when unobserved I could confess.

After about two weeks my opportunity came. It was a Sunday afternoon. Four cell-mates were playing cards with a homemade set of cards. Father Lee and I were sitting close together watching the game. I opened by talking to Father Lee in Latin about card playing. I did this so if afterwards anyone should ask what we had been talking about, we could say we had spoken about the card game.

Then I asked Father Lee if he would hear my confession, since I had not confessed for seven months.

Father Lee said he would. I then made a short confession and the pious priest folded his hands as in the confessional box, closed his eyes in prayer, and quite openly made a sign of the cross as he absolved me. Anyone watching us would have certainly seen we were up to something religious, something unsocialistic, uncommunistic.

I was greatly relieved and thanked this good priest. God bless him!

With the confession over Father Lee said, "Be careful, the fu chu chang (assistant chu chang) is watching us."

This was no sooner said than the fu chu chang shouted at us, demanding to know what we were talking about. Father Lee said that we had been talking about the card game which was true. I had first spoken about the game in preparation for just such a question.

A few days later Father Lee was moved from my cell. I missed him very much. The very presence of a fellow priest was a consolation, even if I hardly ever spoke with him.

A few weeks after this, in the end of the Lenten season, Father Yuan was suddenly brought into our cell. We immediately recognized one another but gave no indication of this.

Father Yuan was ordered, for some reason or other, to leave his cell and join our study classes on this one particular day. He sat near me as I sat near the wall on the edge of the kang, in isolation.

The hour passed, then came our second or last meal of the day around 4:30 P.M. After this we filed out to the latrine.

We went to the latrine twice a day. The first time was about an hour after rising. Outside the cell as we filed along, keeping silent, we were supposed to keep our heads down, with eyes directed to the ground, observing no one else. I kept my eyes down when in view of the Sepo guards, otherwise I took in all the other prisoners I could, to see who were in prison with me, who were in fetters or handcuffs, etc.

On this particular day, some prisoners asked and received permission to collect their clothes which they had hung up in the morning to dry. The others, excepting Father Yuan and me, were detained for some reason or other. Consequently Father Yuan and I returned to our cell.

No sooner were we in the cell than Father Yuan whispered to me in Latin, "Let us give one another conditional absolution. This will stand for our Easter sacrament of penance."

I agreed.

Conditional absolution is given in cases of emergency when a penitent is unable to confess, such as when a large number of soldiers are about to go to battle, in an accident, etc.

Soon the class period opened. I again sat just behind Father Yuan. After about half an hour, I gave him a gentle poke in the back, as I signaled I was about to give him absolution. I noticed the head of the good, pious Chinese priest bend slightly lower and I absolved him. Then I waited and noticed he turned a little towards me, with his right hand hidden under his left arm. I then prayed an act of contrition as he gave me absolution making a sign of the cross with his hidden right hand. So Father Yuan and I received our Easter sacrament of penance in 1952.

About this time I noticed on a few occasions a foreigner among the prisoners. He was of middle age. "He must be a priest," I thought. There was that indefinable characteristic about him that is common in a priest. So one day as I came on him, squatting in the open latrine, I raised my hand and made a little sign of the cross as I gave him absolution. In a moment's time I noticed his hand go up as he made a little sign of the cross, and his lips uttered an absolution for me.

In Ts'ao Lan Tzu and the work prison where I was from September 21, 1954 to July 13, 1955, I gave absolution daily to all the disposed Catholics, and my blessing to all the rest of the prisoners as we gathered, hundreds together, to go to the latrine, or at general assemblies when 4,000 or 5,000 prisoners gathered together. I also did the same to my cell-mates at night on retiring.

So I could multiply accounts of such priestly doings.

God bless those stouthearted priests, Chinese and foreign, and there were many of them, as well as brothers, sisters and Catholic laymen in Ts'ao Lan Tzu and Tzu Hsing Lu prisons, most of whom were thrown into prison for no other reason than that they promoted the Legion of Mary, opposed the separation of the Church from the Bishop of Rome, the Pope, and the like, while they were charged with outrageous, exaggerated crimes.

As I saw these priests, brothers, sisters and Catholic laymen, many in chains, I often thought of the words of Our Blessed Lord:

"Blessed are they who suffer persecution for justice' sake, for theirs is the kingdom of heaven.

"Blessed are you when men reproach you, and persecute you, and, speaking falsely, say all manner of evil against you, for my sake. Rejoice and exult, because your reward is great in heaven; for so did they persecute the prophets who were before you." Matthew V, 10-12.

"When will Easter be this year?" I asked myself in early 1952.

From my arrest on July 25, 1951, to the end of the year, I observed the outstanding feasts: The Assumption of Our Blessed Lady, August 15th; The Nativity of Our Blessed Lady, September 8, which is the anniversary of the foundation of the society of the Missionaries of the Divine Word (S.V.D.); St. Michael's, September 29; St. Teresa of Lisieux, October 3; St. Francis Assisi, October 4; St. Francis Xavier, December 3; the Immaculate Conception, December 8; Christmas; and Circumcision, January 1st.

All these are immovable.

There were many movable feast days approaching, all reckoned on the date of Easter, which changes, year for year: Ash Wednesday, Passion Sunday, Palm Sunday, Holy Week, Easter, Pentecost, Corpus Christi, Trinity Sunday.

Easter is the first Sunday after the first full moon following the vernal equinox, which is March 21st.

I dared not inquire the date of Easter.

So I asked the date of the coming Chinese New Year, usually at the end of our January or the beginning of February. This is a new moon. A full moon is on the fourteenth day following. So I calculated Easter from the Chinese New Year. From Easter, I calculated the entire liturgical period from Ash Wednesday to Trinity Sunday.

In the best manner I could I lived this liturgical period. Since I fasted every day in Ts'ao Lan Tzu, there was no difficulty in perfectly observing the Lenten fast. I commemorated the beautiful feasts, especially Ash Wednesday, Holy Week, Easter, Pentecost, and Trinity, with special meditations and prayers.

Each year in prison, I fixed the Easter and worked out the movable feasts of its period, observing these lovely days.

· 22 ·

Another Denial

"Please give me some more wo tou!" I said to Lei, the chu chang.

By this time, the winter of 1952, I had learned to eat wo tou, the steamed lumps of saltless, unleavened mixture of a low grade of corn or maize, and water.

I was not allowed to take my wo tou from the bowl containing it. It was given me by Lei, the chu chang.

At every meal he gave me a half a wo tou. On finishing this I had to request more. He usually gave me a quarter of a wo tou more with a scowl. He never gave me enough to satisfy my hunger.

My total consumption of wo tou was one and a half a day, at our two meals. The rest of the cell-mates themselves took as much as they wanted.

I also received less pai tsai than the other cell-mates.

Slowly, I was starved.

The communists said that each prisoner receives as much wo tou as he wants. This is a lie! And I am a witness to this lie! For some twelve weeks I was denied enough wo tou to satisfy my hunger!

Let not the communists resort to their hypocritical defense that they did not know of such "infractions of the prison rules!" Such statements have been made and they are downright prevarications, lies in plain English. All that goes on in each cell is reported to the prison authorities who give minute instructions to each chu chang regarding the treatment to be given to each prisoner.

I was greatly reduced in weight. It was evident to all that I was being starved and nothing was done to relieve me. I was being starved to force me into a confession, true or false.

In April 1952, I was shocked one day when the crown on my right, lower, back molar came loose. This crowned tooth served as an anchor for a movable bridge. I had had this crown put on by a Chinese dentist in Peking, a year and four months before, in December 1950.

I wondered how I could get the dental care needed to reset this crown or better to have it replaced by a new one.

As best I could in my poor Chinese, I reported to Lei, the chu chang, what had happened and requested to see the doctor to get dental care.

Lei flew into a rage, shouting that my request was outrageous, and denied me the permission to petition the doctor. The other cell-mates joined in heaping abuse on me—an American imperialist—requesting dental care!

When opportunity offered itself and I had an interview with the prison physician at Ts'ao Lan Tzu and often later at Tzu Hsing Lu work prison, I requested dental care for this loose crown as well as the other teeth that pained me. But never was I given dental care. The most I received were some tablets on two or three occasions at Tzu Hsing Lu prison, to stop the pain.

From April 1952, to my release from prison September 10, 1955, a period of 3 years and 6 months, I suffered repeatedly from prolonged, and at times severe, toothaches, without any relief. Chewing was most painful.

This was another cunning manner in which I was tortured.

In the winter of 1952, I suffered much anguish of mind over my false confession of being an F.B.I. agent and of falsely accusing confreres out of China, out of reach of the cruel Chinese communists, of being F.B.I. agents.

"Suppose the countries in which these confreres live were taken over by communists, these confreres would be arrested as F.B.I. men because I had accused them of being such," I thought.

All communist countries share the intelligence they get, especially do they report their intelligence to their masters in Moscow, Russia.

I decided that at the first opportunity, I would deny these false confessions. I felt I was especially bound to deny the false accusation of my confreres even if this cost me my life. I would deny being an F.B.I. agent and all subsequent related false confessions.

The opportunity came.

In late March 1952, a court official called me to the little office in the prison compound for interviewing prisoners.

He opened up, "You are an F.B.I. agent. Are you not?"

"I am not an F.B.I. agent!" I said without a moment's hesitation.

"What!" he shouted, "You deny you are an F.B.I. man after having confessed that you are!"

"Yes," I said, "my confession of being an F.B.I. man was false and all my other confessions relating to this were false."

"Did you tell this to your judge?" he said.

"Not yet," I replied, "I have not had an opportunity."

After shouting at me, pressing me to hold to my false confession of being an F.B.I. agent, he then proceeded with his other business.

On returning to my cell, I felt greatly relieved, but thought that I would soon be shot. This was my seventh denial of being an F.B.I. agent and I had no doubt that it was immediately reported to my judge.

A week or so later, I was called out for a night court session. A new judge was sitting on the bench. He wore a perpetual sneer. He was quite young, looking like a young man of the late twenties.

Evidently he was acquainted with my denial of being an F.B.I. man.

He opened the session with the statement "You are an agent of the U. S. Government."

"I am not an agent of the U. S. Government!" I snapped back.

The judge became furious, shouted at me and pounded the desk, but I held to my statement.

"But you are a spy," he eventually said.

I hesitated, then replied, "Yes, I am a spy." I had formerly said I was a spy. Everyone is a spy according to the Chinese communists. Everyone who exercises any sense perception is collecting intelligence. Everyone who expresses any ideas, by talking, writing, moving the hands, and the like, is passing on intelligence.

This may sound fantastic.

It seems fantastic, but it is true.

So I admitted I was a spy.

The judge then proceeded with the main questions for which he had called me.

had been arrested on the same day, 25 July, 1951. The prison authorities missed fire when they put Luke and me together. We sympathized with each other, not openly of course, but in a manner each other understood. He did shout at me a few times, but with a few exceptions in such a subdued manner that his shouting consoled me instead of punishing me.

In early July, my regular judge of court No. 4 called me for the first time since early January of the same year, 1952.

He opened by inquiring about my thoughts of the past half year, since he had last called me.

Shielding myself by my ignorance of Chinese, I replied that as I knew little or no Chinese, I was unable to understand the newspaper articles when they were read or to follow the discussions in the study periods.

"But what have you been thinking about?" he pressed.

"I expected to be deported," I replied.

"You expected to be deported? Why did you expect such?"

"You had led me to believe that if I confessed, I would be deported. Wang who had been sent by the court to 'help' me, told me on many occasions that I would be deported if I confessed. And I have confessed everything that could be considered a crime in the eyes of the government. Therefore, I expected to be deported," I said.

"You are a fool! You are deceiving yourself. No spy will be deported, unless he enjoys diplomatic immunity, and you do not enjoy such. Drop this foolish idea."

This was a shock to me. I was quite speechless, then said, "But you gave me to understand and Wang who represented you, clearly promised me to be deported, if I confessed, and I confessed."

"The 'People's' government has changed its policy. No spy, as you, will ever be deported."

"So there you are," I thought, "first this government promises to deport you if you confess. Then you confess and are told the government has changed its policy. You will not be released. Communists do not keep their promises. They are not to be trusted."

"What else has been on your mind?" he said.

"I corrected the false confession I made that I was an F.B.I. agent."

"What!" he shouted. "We have recorded evidence that you are an F.B.I. agent. You cannot deny it."

"What possible recorded evidence could the court have?" I thought. "He is bluffing me, or the court has distorted a piece of evidence. But the court, this communist court, this prejudiced, anti-American, anti-Catholic court decides the value of the evidence that comes into their hands. What chances do I have?"

"But I am not an F.B.I. agent," I said, "and never was one."

So the farce continued. The judge shouted at me, threatened to shoot me, insisted that he had evidence, recorded evidence, against me. I maintained that my denial was true.

He ended by ordering me to return to my cell and reconsider my denial.

The Good Sisters of Fu Jen

ON RETURNING to my cell from the court, I was dejected by the realization that the government planned not to deport me. I was, however, pleased that I had persevered in my denial of being an F.B.I. man.

I had deep misgiving, however, over the judge's declaration that the court had recorded evidence of my being an F.B.I. agent. "Tenuous evidence," I thought, "that the court alone would evaluate."

Some months later the judge accused me of supplying intelligence over the phone to an American vice consul. He said I had investigated a certain priest of Fu Jen University (whose name he gave) and reported the results to the vice consul who, he said, was an F.B.I. man. The particular priest, a member of the Divine Word Missionaries, was on the staff of Fu Jen University and had left for the U. S. for advanced university studies. The U. S. consulate actually had called me on the phone, inquiring about him, asking for my confirmation or denial of his being on the Fu Jen staff and a character report on him.

As the rector of Fu Jen University and the Fu Jen community, I was the first to be approached about this matter and I informed the vice consul there and then over the phone, that the priest in question was what he claimed to be and I gave him a good and true character recommendation. At this time, my phone calls were tapped and recorded. Hence, I concluded that the so-called recorded evidence the court had of me being an F.B.I. agent, was the recorded conversation I had with this vice consul over this priest.

On returning to my cell after this court session, Tito, the Russian-Serbian chu chang, Wang, the Chinese merchant and Luke, the foreign physician, all three English-speaking, started to work on me, to "help" me retract my denial.

For some days these three pressed, urged and lectured me. Tito fumed and shouted around. Wang was a close second. I remember how this returned student from the U.S.A., throwing his arms in the air, shouted, "Rigney, you are an enemy of my country, the 'People's' China. I will treat you as an American soldier in Korea, fighting my country. If I had a gun here, I would shoot you!"

Luke, the foreign physician, joined in a half-hearted manner, advising me to look at my problem from the "People's" point of view.

At last, worn out, I again admitted I was an F.B.I. agent.

Then followed court sessions for several days and nights, in which the judge pressed me to confess more and to explain why I denied my confession.

The cell-mates continued this torture when I was not in court. Once in desperation, I said, "I denied because in my heart I know I am not an F.B.I. man."

At this, there was an outburst of fury, cursing and lecturing from the cell-mates that lasted for days until I retracted this, the ninth denial.

I was truly wretched.

In February of this year, 1952, the court instructed me to write a note to the sisters who sent supply packages to the other Divine Word Missionaries in the prison of Ts'ao Lan Tzu. This in a way was bad news since it indicated that my confreres in Fu Jen were either arrested or deported. On the other hand I welcomed the needed supplies the sisters might send. So I wrote a note to these sisters, the Holy Ghost Missionary Sisters (S.Sp.S.), who had taught at Fu Jen University and had been in charge of the Women's college there.*

In about a week, these good German and Chinese Sisters sent me a package containing shou chih (toilet paper), one or two handkerchiefs, soap, salt and about a pound of assorted food: sandwiches, a little meat, peanuts. More they were not allowed to send.

Every three weeks thereafter, on a Monday, these sisters sent me a package usually of shou chih and soap. No food was allowed. These packages were little in themselves but great in the message they conveyed; that the sisters were still in Peking, that they still thought and prayed for me, that I was not entirely abandoned, that I still had a few friends who were able and willing to help me. God bless those good sisters! Every three weeks they prepared my package, and brought it to the prison, standing in line, awaiting their turn to hand over my package to the rude, uncouth communist Sepo who freely abused them.

They risked their safety for me.

How can I ever forget them?

How can I ever repay them?

I felt they were the last friends I had!

I knew my relatives and friends would have done anything to help me, but the barbarous, hypocritical, perfidious, inhuman disciples of Karl Marx prevented them.

I looked forward and counted the days for the arrival of these packages, these messages of fidelity.

Then one day they stopped. One third Monday in October 1952, no package was delivered to me. The officer came and

---

* The American members of Holy Ghost Missionary Sisters had already been sent back to Holy Ghost Convent, Techny, Illinois, by Father Rigney.

threw into the cell packages for other prisoners, but none for me. He gave no explanation.

Communists seldom give explanations.

Communists are forever pressing their victims and their opponents to give explanations.

Communists do not play their games squarely.

Communists do not keep the rules that they demand their victims and opponents keep.

Shame on the communists!

Shame on their dirty tricks—their dirty tactics!

When these packages stopped, I feared that the good German sisters were either imprisoned or deported and the good Chinese sisters were imprisoned or prevented from helping me. I worried very much for these sisters. I inquired why the packages ceased to be delivered, but the disciples of Karl Marx persisted in giving no explanations.

On the other hand, I later learned the Sepo guards refused to accept packages from the sisters for me. No explanations were given. The sisters then thought I was dead.

My relatives, my friends thought I was dead.

The communists sat back and smiled.

All sadists smile at the sufferings of their victims.

One word from the Chinese communists would have saved the heartaches of my relatives, but what do the Chinese communists care about human sufferings as long as they can rule, as long as they are the neo-aristocracy, the neo-nobility of China.

The chilly weather of the Peking October came, in that 1952. Again I suffered from the cold. In the spring of 1952, on the advice of the chu chang, I had sent all my warm, winter clothing to the sisters to keep for me and mend for me.

Now the good sisters were not allowed to send me anything, either shou chih, soap or winter clothing and bedding. I suffered from the cold. The damp cells were not heated until late November. I was issued Japanese cotton jacket and pants, but soon these were insufficient. My feet moreover were always cold.

Finally, I was allowed to purchase woolen socks and a cotton padded hat. Purchasing these brought my supply of money down.

In the June of 1953, my money was low and Peking prices were high. A bar of laundry soap about half the size of a bar of American Family laundry soap cost the equivalent of 15 U. S. cents.

Furthermore, I did not know how long I would be in prison or if I would be moved away from my Peking prison where I had lived and could best get money, if at all.

So I asked permission to write to a certain priest of influence in Peking, whom I had aided, for money.

In a week's time the prison officer told me I should not write to this priest for aid since he would not help a reactionary like me, but I could write to the sisters who had formerly sent me supplies, and ask them to send me shou chih, soap and even some food, but no money.

This was a doubly good announcement: first, it conveyed that happy news that the Fu Jen Sisters, Holy Ghost Missionary Sisters (S.Sp.S.), were still in Peking and secondly, I could get supplies.

I wrote to the good sisters.

On the following Monday, the officer brought me first a bundle of shou chih, soap, etc. and then to my great surprise a big basket of food—all from the good sisters.

It was during a class period and consequently, I was not allowed to examine these two packages.

I sat on the edge of the kang, looking at the big basket of food and could see white bread, sausages, a jar of butter, sugar, and the like.

I was deeply moved. My eyes soon became moistened. The

food was simply wonderful but what was infinitely more wonderful and consoling was the message of confidence in me, of loyalty and sincere Christian charity it silently conveyed to me.

"The grandest creatures God made after He made His Blessed Mother were Catholic nuns and the finest of these were the Holy Ghost Missionary Sisters!" I thought.

Three or four of these wonderful baskets of food were sent at intervals of three weeks, then they stopped.

As usual no explanations were given.

Only shou chih and soap came.

Then even these stopped in October 1953.

And no explanations were given.

I concluded that since the "magnanimity" of the "People's" government, which allowed such wonderful food packages, failed to move me to confess and accuse others as the Reds wanted me to, all packages were again stopped.

Shortly before this I had been ordered to give detailed reports in duplicate about every member of the U. S. Consulate in Peking. I was told to give the biography, including education, hobbies; the social connections; espionage activities; unsavory, scandalous conduct; etc. of each.

I gave good and true reports about all these I knew. And there were no scandals to report to the communist scandalmongers. The staff of the Consulate was certainly of high moral quality and integrity. I felt proud of them, indeed.

I could have helped myself by scribbling pages of false, salacious rubbish. Though untrue, it would have made the kind of calumnious propaganda the communists like to publish. But I did not, and consequently was evidently punished. This was just one more demonstration of the dirty tactics of the Chinese communists.

·25·

The Last Denial

"I AM NOT and never was a member of the F.B.I. (Federal Bureau of Investigation) of the U. S. A. government," I wrote with a steel pen on the official manila paper of the prison. At the end I wrote the date, October 13, 1952, signing my name in English and in Chinese, and finishing by rubbing ink on my right index finger and impressing my finger print to this statement. In this manner I dated and signed all statements I made in prison.

My cell-mates had been pressing me, tou chenging me for many days to confess why I had denied my F.B.I. confession.

"I denied it because I was ashamed of disgracing the priesthood," I said.

"What other reason?"

"I was ashamed of disgracing my Church."

"What other reason? All you say is only a composition."

"I was ashamed of disgracing my religious society."

"Nonsense! Stop talking that way! Why did you deny your confession?"

"Because the denial was the truth!" I said.

"What!" Tito bellowed, "What did you say! Write that down and get shot!"

While I wrote, my six cell-mates gathered around me, shouting and jumping, blaspheming God and cursing my mother and me, in English and Chinese.

Tito, Wang, and Luke were the loudest. The first two were furious. Luke had to chime in to save himself and even me from more persecution that would otherwise have been meted out to us for being friends. We could hate each other, but we could not manifest any brotherly love towards each other. Hell is like that—damned souls hate each other, never love each other. And Ts'ao Lan Tzu was modeled after hell. Its planners must have been inspired by one well acquainted with hell.

Wang, the merchant, showered me with voluminous curses as he saw what he thought was the ground for his release slip away.

Tito, the Russian-Serbian, bellowed and behaved like a wild man as he realized that he had failed in his assignment.

Luke, the physician, shouted but in an unconvincing manner. I had a feeling of satisfaction that now Luke would not believe me an F.B.I. agent, if he ever had, because it would be foolhardy to write and sign such a statement if it were not true. Such a repudiation means requesting severe punishment, even death, if the government declares it false.

I think I was the calmest in the cell although what I was doing placed me in the position of the most danger. I was calm because my conscience was at peace. I had for the tenth and, what I then firmly resolved to be, the last time repudiated the false confession I had made fourteen months before, that I was an F.B.I. agent. I thought I might get shot for this or receive a long prison sentence of twenty or more years, but come what may, I was back on the path of truth. Death or a long prison sentence was preferred to the ignominy of a life of falsehood.

When the ink of the fingerprint dried, I handed my written repudiation and denial of my false F.B.I. confession to Tito.

He took it, then shouted, "Why did you make the false confession?"

"To deceive the government," I replied.

On a former occasion when the same question was asked, I replied, "To avoid being tortured." I was severely tou chenged for this because it was the wrong answer. The "People's" government never tortures anyone, according to their statement. But their statements generally must be understood in the opposite meaning.

"Why did you want to deceive the government?" Tito roared, pounding on the little table on the kang.

No matter what a prisoner answers, there is always one more question the disciples of Karl Marx hurl at a victim being questioned: "Why did you say (or do) that?" There is just no end to a discussion with them until you confess some heinous crime, true or false, or else accuse others, truly or falsely.

The entire cell was in an uproar. I was being tou chenged. All the cell-mates had gathered around me, shouting at me, cursing me, questioning me, as they pointed their fingers into my face, while I sat on the kang.

It was in the evening.

Suddenly the door opened and the officer ordered all the cell-mates to go to the movie that was soon to be shown. Never had I been allowed to attend one of the movies or stage performances that came every month or so.

We all filed out into a line in the court. A count of the prisoners was made. We then were led to a cold hall and ordered to sit on the dirty floor.

The movie was a propaganda film against the Americans fighting in Korea. The clapping of the prisoners shocked me. Every time an American plane was depicted as shot down, or an American soldier was shown falling dead, or corpses of killed American soldiers appeared, there was loud clapping of hands of the prisoners. I sat there without clapping, but this only invited more persecution, since Sepo guards kept sharp eyes to detect if any prisoner failed to join in the clapping in the so-called "free" China.

On the following morning, I was ordered to sit motionless on the kang with my legs crossed and my head against the wall. Whenever I moved, as I sat in this position which was especially painful for my legs, the cell-mates shouted at me and hit me in the back.

From rising to retiring, excepting for meals and going to the toilet, I had to sit in this cramped, painful position for eight days.

Besides praying, I watched the sunlight creep along the wall. If I went to sleep, the cell-mates shouted at me, cursing me, ordering me to stay awake.

This torture was to induce me to confess what I had been hiding by making a false confession.

The officer said no false confession is ever made in Ts'ao Lan Tzu unless to hide a bigger crime. Now, I was pressed to confess the big crime I had been hiding by my false F.B.I. confession.

I insisted I had attempted to hide no crime.

In these days I told Tito that I had not been given to lying, and the false confession I had made, brought me much mental anguish.

"You Protestant ministers and Catholic priests are professional liars!" Tito shouted. "You have not the slightest idea of the truth. You, Rigney, a Catholic priest, are an habitual liar. You are a very low character. You are a spy, worse than a murderer. You are the worst, most depraved character I have ever met!

"In Harbin there used to be a secret society known as the Sadists. To be eligible to join this society, one must either have murdered someone in cold blood or have raped a little girl below 7 years of age. You, Rigney, are guilty of worse crimes than murder and rape. Therefore, you are eligible to join the Sadists of Harbin."

For one year I listened to insults of this type from Tito.

26

Tou Cheng and Self Criticism

FROM THE early part of December 1952, until the early part of January, 1953, I was subjected to daily tou chenging and self criticism. Tito, the Russian-Serbian chu chang led this attempt to make me either retract my denial of my false F.B.I. confession or confess some other spying connection.

"That — — — Rigney," Tito said to Luke, "is an American agent who joined the S.V.D.'s (Latin abbreviation for Divine Word Missionaries) to get control of its American branch. The U. S. government obtained control of the American S.V.D. in this way. Rigney controls them for the U. S. government. He is no priest. He is an American agent disguised as a priest. You d—— fool, Luke, can't you see that!"

So Tito went on talking to Luke in a subdued voice as if he were telling him something confidential. But he spoke loud enough for me to hear him. In this way Tito suggested to me what I should confess. He reported and received instructions at least once a day from the prison authorities concerning me.

As a matter of fact, I joined the Divine Word Missionaries as a student in 1918, when I was 17 years old. It does seem quite incredible for one of that age to be a qualified, highly trained agent but the communists are not much concerned with the credibility or incredibility of statements. They are interested in melodramatic confessions or accusations. Whether they are true or false, libelous or not, is of quite a secondary consideration.

Day after day, I was obliged to reveal my thoughts to this

group of three. To have refused to at least attempt this, or to have kept silent, would have brought on worse tortures. The only alternatives to the many and diabolically cunning tortures of the communists of Peking was either losing one's mind or getting shot. In the case of the former, new kinds of tortures were substituted for the old ones, as I saw when cell-mates who had gone stark mad underwent tortures. In the case of the latter, when a prisoner sought execution as a surcease, he was dealt tortures from which death was truly a relief, as my judge explained to me one day.

"What do you think of communists?" Tito bellowed.

"I do not and never will accept their philosophy of Marxist communism, because it is based on dialectical materialism and as a Catholic, I cannot accept this materialistic philosophy. I would prefer death to being a communist," I said.

"You are using diplomatic language, you liar! Why don't you speak out and say you hate the communists."

"I do not hate communists. It is unchristian to hate anyone. I do hate communism, dialectical materialistic philosophy that constitutes the fundamentals of communism. But I do not hate communists, on the contrary, I pray every day for the spiritual welfare of the communists of this prison, of Peking and of all China, but I hate their philosophy."

"What is the difference, Rigney, call a spade a spade. You hate communists.

"You also hate the government of China, you Wall Street imperialist," he added.

"I hate the communist aspect of the government of China."

"You hate the Chinese communist government!"

Then he jotted down in his notebook that Rigney says he hates the communists. Rigney says he hates the People's government of China.

So Tito's standing was enhanced by reporting that he had succeeded in wringing such incriminating statements out of Rigney, the American imperialist.

"Now Rigney, tomorrow you must expose your thoughts about us three: Wang, Luke and me. You will have all night to examine your thoughts," Tito said one night in this month or more, of the ordeal I was going through.

"Well Rigney," Tito said with a sneer after he, Wang and Luke gathered around me the next morning, "what do you think of me?" He evidently thought I would fear to be frank and as a consequence he could deal out to me plenty of his insults, shoutings, and the like tortures.

"You, Tito, are an opportunist," I said as he winced under this unexpected exposure.

"'You served with the communists in their 'Liberation army' when this was advantageous.

"You then served with the Kuomintang when this was to your advantage.

"You later had close connections and made money on the Americans, some of whom were in the pay of the U. S. government, when this was to your advantage.

"Now you are doing your best to serve the communists again because they are in control.

"If the Americans would return, you would be back with them, making money off of them.

"You are an opportunist. It is not pleasant for me to tell you this but you asked for it. You ordered me to sincerely and truthfully reveal my thoughts about you and I have."

In a fit of rage Tito pounded the kang and shouted, "Rigney, if the Americans would ever come back, I would kill you with a wooden dagger, the bloodiest and most painful way I know to kill you. And the Marines would find me weeping over your dead body!"

Thus my month of tou chenging, self-criticism went on. Tito went to great lengths telling me, over and over again, "Rigney you are an innate liar. It is time you started to tell the truth. You are not fit to confess. As a matter of fact the government has not decided whether to allow you to confess or to shoot you. As you are now going, you will never leave Ts'ao Lan Tzu alive, except for a short one-way journey to the Tien Ch'iao, the execution grounds."

Wang was a close second to Tito as a master of the "art" of insulting and torturing and I was his target.

All this may seem trifling but to a prisoner of Ts'ao Lan Tzu it was not.

In the Autumn of 1951, the court questioned me about my knowledge of the Chinese Third Party Government (which was neither Kuomintang nor Communist) program of the U. S. A. for China.

The judge accused me of being an American Government agent to contact Chinese leaders for the development of this Third Party.

It was true that I knew Dr. Hu Shih, Chancellor of the National Peking University and member of the Board of Trustees of Fu Jen University. He had been ambassador to the United States and was a noted scholar and diplomat.

In the spring of 1948, I called on Dr. Hu Shih, as a member of The Board of Trustees of Fu Jen, to consult with him about the future policy of Fu Jen.

I must suppose that at least one of the servants of Dr. Hu Shih reported to the communists about my visit with Dr. Hu Shih.

I had also attended two receptions of General Li Chung-Jen, while he was head of the North China Government under the nationalists.

Both Dr. Hu Shih and General Li Chung-Jen were in the U. S. A. as reputed leaders of the Third Party.

I had likewise attended two banquets given by General Fu Tso-I, the last Nationalist commander of Peiping as well as the last head of the North China Government of Nationalist China.

Fu Tso-I had been an outstanding anti-communist, a capable military strategist and a pro-American. In 1949, he went over, lock, stock and barrel, to the communist side, surrendering Peiping, his large armies and huge military supplies. As his reward he became cabinet Minister of Water Conservancy of the communist government.

I also knew Ho Sze-yuan, Mayor of Peiping 1946-1948. He had been Military Governor of Shantung. In 1949, he went over to the communist side in Peiping.

Hu-Shih, Li Chung-Jen, Fu Tso-I and Ho Sze-yuan, were regarded as liberal and potential leaders of a Third Party Government.

I told the court I knew nothing special or particular about the Third Party Government movement beyond knowing the above mentioned outstanding Chinese.

Later in the winter of 1953, I was called to the judge who demanded that I confess all my activities on behalf of the Third Party Government.

I told him I knew nothing beyond what I had told him before in 1951.

"What! You liar! Stop your lying!" he barked. "You have been in prison for almost two years and have not yet reformed! You do not understand the government's policy. You know much about the American attempt to form a Third Party Government in China. I see you do not want to help yourself."

So he went on, abusing me, for at least one hour.

I held my ground, truthfully stating that I knew nothing about this Third Party beyond what was commonly known.

27

An Unforgetting, Forgotten Prisoner

"STALIN IS SICK," Tito said as he told me the message broad-casted over the prison loud speaker system on a morning in early March 1953.

"Stalin is sick?" I thought. "What does that mean?"

In some parts of the world when a leader takes ill, no public announcements are made. When he dies, an announcement is made that he is sick. Sometime later, usually a few days, when the deceased leader's party have taken measures to secure themselves, a notice is published that the leader has passed away. "Stalin must be dead," I thought.

A few hours later, around noon, there was another message broadcasted. All the other cell-mates looked very solemn. I asked Tito what the message was.

"Marshal Stalin is dead," he said in mournful cadences.

It seemed all the prisoners were stunned and on their guard.

The large cloth covered window towards the courtyard was opened in our cell, as in a nearby cell where an American woman was kept prisoner. A special Sepo guard marched back and forth between the cells where this American woman and I were held. This seemed to me to be a special guard to watch us two Americans and detect any of our possible derogatory remarks about the deceased dictator or signs of jubilation over his being called to judgment. I sat particularly quiet.

As I expected, Tito said on the following day, "Well Rigney, what thoughts are on your mind over the passing of Marshal Stalin?"

I formulated a statement such as I thought President Eisenhower, or Secretary of State Dulles would make in their official diplomatic messages of condolence to the Kremlin.

"The passing of Stalin is a great loss to the people of the Soviet Union," I replied.

"Rigney," Tito said as he appeared to be on the verge of breaking down with grief, "the passing of Marshal Stalin is a great loss to all the people of the entire world."

I was relieved that I had hurdled this loaded question with such ease.

A few days later, all prisoners had to stand silent and at attention for five minutes, while cannons in the Red Square before the Tien An Men (the main entrance to the old imperial palace) fired a salute during the memorial services held there for Stalin.

The days passed. I continued to be isolated, set in a corner by Tito, not allowed to play cards in free time.

Spring came and with it new hopes of being released. The United Nations command in Korea opened negotiations with the Korean and Chinese communists to exchange prisoners.

I hoped that we civilian prisoners of nations participating in the U.N.O. Army would be released.

In early July, my judge called me to a court session. Again he asked me how I had gotten on during the passed year and what I was thinking about.

I told him I was pleased over the exchange of prisoners in Korea.

He told me to harbor no illusionary hopes of being included among those exchanged. "The Americans," he told me, "were forced by the 'people' of the world to exchange prisoners. This was a great victory for the people. The stronger the 'people's' China gets, the more severely it will deal with criminals like you."

He then gave me questions to guide me in writing up my

confession. He wanted it done on special paper in a great hurry. Luke said, "There must be some special reason why the judge has set a deadline for your confession, Rigney. It looks like your case is being prepared for settlement."

I worked hard four days and nights without interruption writing, writing this confession, in carefully written hand, writing with a steel pen. I held to my denial of being an F.B.I. agent and was allowed to write this confession without confessing membership in this organization.

Thus my two year's struggle over my confession of being an F.B.I. agent closed with my tenth repudiation made in October 1952, being, at least, tentatively accepted. I felt this was a victory for me.

In the midst of writing this confession, Tito was told one midnight to pack up his belongings. He had said the court had decided to grant him clemency because he had confessed well, accused others well and kept the prison rules. He also left some of his food for the cell-mates: an indication he was being released.

After Tito left, to the relief of all, four chu changs succeeded each other until a nasty, effeminate character, named Teng (pronounced "Dung"), took over.

Teng was a selfish character. On Sundays, the only cards that could be played were the kind he liked. And he selected players that suited him. He declared me undesirable: an American imperialist and a Vatican imperialist.

He contradicted me wherever and whenever he could. Nothing I did was acceptable. I could never wash the floor properly. No matter how careful I was, no matter how often I rinsed the wash rags, there was always something wrong with my work.

Once, by accident I spilled one or two drops of drinking water on another cell-mate's shou chih (toilet paper). This was nothing since the water soon dried, doing no damage to the toilet paper. Teng, however, flew into a rage and began shouting at me, insulting me, cursing me. At this, of course, the rest of the cell-mates also began doing the same, bellowing at me, insulting and cursing me.

Teng was my chu chang for about six months and they were bitter six months.

On top of the persecution of the cell-mates, two events occurred that dejected me: the escape (or release, as claimed by the communists) of some 26,000 Chinese and Korean prisoners. The Chinese communists were furious over this. They accused the Americans of abducting these prisoners and forcing them into the armies of the Republic of Korea and the National Government of China. I thought we American civilian prisoners would have to suffer for this loss of face of the communists. We were victims of the cold war.

The second event was the release of some 22,000 prisoners by the U.N.O. staff in Korea.

The Chinese communists were incensed by this. It was a great loss of face for them. They again accused the Americans of abducting these prisoners and forcing them into the armies of the Republic of Korea and the National Government of China.

It seemed to me that we civilian American prisoners were forgotten. There was evidently much interest and pains taken by U.N.O. and especially the Americans to secure the release of these prisoners who had taken up arms against the U.S.A. But what was being done for us civilian Americans who had never taken up arms against U.N.O. or the U.S.A.? I realized, however, that the U.S.A. was in a position in which they could do little or nothing for us.

I could never forget my relatives and friends, the society to which I belonged—the Divine Word Missionaries—and my country. But it seemed they had forgotten me or were unable to help me.

I felt as if I were the unforgetting, forgotten man. I recalled how quickly people in Peking forgot about priests I had known who had been arrested before me. In a few months they were quite forgotten by all but their own confreres.

I was an unforgetting, forgotten prisoner.

·28·

Drowsiness

"Rui Ko Ni! Are you sleeping again! Wake up! What do you mean by disobeying the rules again!"

From the autumn of 1951, when my daily night court sessions came to an end to the summer of 1955, when I was placed in solitary confinement, I found it difficult to stay awake throughout the day and evenings and frequently fell asleep.

In the last eight weeks of my imprisonment while in solitary confinement, away from the persecution of my cell-mates, I had no difficulty in staying awake.

Before this, it was most fatiguing to sit, hour after hour, throughout the day and evening, in a corner of the cell, day after day, week after week, month after month, one year, two years, three years—isolated, shunned and persecuted by cell-mates, like a leper, an outcast, a despised, discredited individual who had lost all face, who once had been influential and respected but now was powerless, a condemned criminal to be shunned; a vile reptile to be crushed and most of all a valuable, wonderful object, a scapegoat, on which an opportunistic prisoner could vent his hatred, to demonstrate to the communist government how pro-communist he had become.

As I learned from the statements of many prisoners, the average cell-mate thought about me along such lines as the following: "This Rigney, look at him! He is a foreigner, an American! He is so thin, weak and helpless!

"He is of no use!

"He cannot profit me!

"Perhaps in the past, his friendship would have been valuable. He could have given me a job or recommended me to a friend of his for a job. He could have given me direct assistance as he did countless students of Fu Jen University and other needy people.

"But that is all of the past! What can he do now? Now! The present!

"Nothing! He is an American and America is no longer powerful. She is losing the Korean War, her air force is poor, her army fears to fight. America is a paper tiger. The Soviet Union is now the most powerful country in the world. Even the 'People's' China is dealing the armed forces of the U. S. A. an ignominious defeat in Korea.

"Rigney is also a Catholic, and the Catholic Church is lined up with Wall Street against communism!

"He is a sheng fu (priest). Formerly a sheng fu could help me whether I was a Catholic or not, but now a sheng fu is useless.

"I must look to myself and do what I can for my own present and future needs.

"The communists now control China. For a long time I believed America would prevent the communists from gaining China and later, after the Reds came, I thought America would overthrow them. But all my ideas of the power of the U. S. A. have been wrong. The communists are strong and will remain in power.

"I must support the communists and forget about America who will never assume the position of influence in China she formerly had.

"The Chinese communists hate America and the Catholic Church. Therefore, I must show hatred of all things American and Catholic. I must show hatred of Americans and Catholics, especially Catholic priests who are not pro-communist.

"Rigney is an American and a Catholic priest and he refuses to come over to the communist side. Therefore, I must not show any sympathy with him; on the contrary, I will improve my standing with the prison and communist authorities if I show hatred of him!

"I will show hatred of him."

The average prisoner was daily subjected to communist propaganda. In time he came completely under this influence since there was no free press to acquaint him with the other side of current questions.

He was in an intellectual gas chamber, in which pure air is slowly but surely replaced by carbon monoxide gas. In time he comes under the influence of the poisonous fumes and falls into a stupor, unconscious of reality around him. Finally he dies,—mentally.

Can anyone be surprised then if such prisoners become brainwashed, especially if they lack a solid philosophical foundation as most prisoners I knew did?

So there I was, isolated in a corner of the cell, with cellmates tense in their eagerness to focus their wrath on me, an "unreformed" American Catholic priest.

Daily, under the mental strain of Ts'ao Lan Tzu and later Tzu Hsing Lu prison life, drowsiness came over me during the day or evening. I fought it off but usually my worn-out mental and nervous faculties succumbed to sleep.

Sometimes I woke without having been detected.

Often, I was not so fortunate, but some zealous cell-mate discovered this "crime" and shouted "Rui Ko Ni, are you sleeping again! Wake up! What do you mean by disobeying the rules again!"

Then usually followed a sound volley of abusive language, bellowed at me by the chu chang and cell-mates.

At times, I was subjected to a tou cheng, in which I was

accused of sleeping because I was tired as a result of worrying over unconfessed crimes, and the like. What were these crimes? What was I hiding? I was asked.

Explanations of mental exhaustion were repudiated and only precipitated more vehement tou chenging.

The best way was simply to say nothing, to weather the storm. But until the middle of 1955, I suffered from this inability to stay awake during the ten hours of daily, so-called study periods, or during the many and long kai huai (meetings) or lectures by the prison authorities on kai ts'ao (reformation).

This was especially the case in 1952, 1953, and up to September 21, 1954 when I was sentenced and removed to Tzu Hsing Lu prison.

·29·

On the Verge of a Mental Breakdown

"Sign and fingerprint this,"the judge said as he threw back to me the statement I had written.

I had been called to a court session with a strange judge who spoke English. He had asked me about the Catholic students of Fu Jen University. My reports about them were not incriminating. The judge, as usual in such cases, was angry. After all, he was not so much interested in a true statement about these good Catholic students as he was in getting grounds, true or false, to persecute them, to destroy the Catholic faith in them, to turn them on their former teachers at Fu Jen, to turn them against their bishops and priests.

After about two hours of fruitless questioning, he ordered me to make a written statement there and then, in the courtroom.

I sat on a bench before a small tea table and began to write with the steel pen and ink, on the cheap manila paper provided by the court.

It seemed difficult to write.

"I must write," I thought. I exerted unusual effort to write. "I must write something." So I wrote, abbreviating many words ordinarily not abbreviated.

"Let me see what you have written," the judge said as I finished.

"Write this over!" he shouted after glancing at the statement and throwing it back to me, "and write clearly. I cannot read this."

So I sat down again and copied my statement, making efforts to write clearly and without the unconventional abbreviations I had used. On finishing, I handed my statement to the judge. He took it and looked at it.

"Sign and fingerprint this," he said as he threw my statement back to me.

I signed in Chinese and English as usual.

Then I did a very strange thing.

Raising my finger in the air, I went through the motions of rolling my right index finger tip as if the ink pad were suspended in the air.

"This will do," I thought, "this is all make-believe anyway."

Then I rolled my finger tip on my statement, next to my signature, and returned the statement to the judge who was absorbed with a book or some paper.

He took one glance, grew angry, threw first my statement back to me, then the ink pad at his side, shouting, "Fingerprint this! I told you to fingerprint it!"

In bewilderment, I then properly fingerprinted my statement.

On my way to my cell, a fear came over me, a new kind of fear I had never experienced in my life.

"What have I done?" I thought. "Lifting my hand in the air and rolling my finger for ink that was not there! This is not the way a normal man acts! Can it be that I am losing my mind?"

I feared to answer this question.

Then I remembered back 38 years to the days when I had studied Shakespeare's King Lear in my preparatory seminary days. King Lear realized he was losing his mind. I remembered a footnote stating that often a person loosing his mind realizes that he is going insane.

This memory frightened me more.

On returning to my cell, I took my place on the kang in a corner of the cell, where I sat, that day in January 1954, two years and six months after my arrest, and reviewed my conduct in the courtroom.

The cell-mates told me in those days that I spoke in my sleep as I had never done before.

It was difficult for me to make up my mind to do anything. Often I sat in my corner, an isolated prisoner, especially despised and persecuted by the other cell-mates, unable to arouse myself to get up, for instance, and walk to the other end of the cell to look for my notebook which I had left there.

One of these days, the members of the cell were ordered to prepare for a bath. The other cell-mates quickly got their soap, if they had any, and a little towel that served for a wash rag and after being wrung for a towel.

I sat there, on the edge of the kang, motionless and indifferent.

"Rigney, do you have your towel?" the English-speaking cell-mate who was allowed to speak to me in English, asked me.

"I am prepared," I said.

When we were ordered to leave for bath, I joined the cell-mates, without soap or towel.

In the bathing pool, I simply splashed water on myself for a few minutes, then went to the room where our clothes were heaped on the floor. I was wet and shivering from the January cold. In this condition I dressed and returned to my cell, walking about 1000 feet.

I was happy that no one saw that I had had no towel, else I would have been tou chenged by all the cell-mates for not taking one. The cell-mates took every opportunity they could to contradict me, shout at me, tou cheng me, the American imperialist, the Catholic priest.

Several incidents as the above occurred. For some of them

I was punished when I should have received kindness. Teng, the chu chang, however, was too selfish to forego an opportunity to advance himself at my expense.

On another occasion I was given a paper, a report to write for the court. I could hardly write, my hand was so unsteady. But I wrote out the paper and handed it to the English-speaking cell-mate to be translated into Chinese.

At one glance he said, "Rigney, your handwriting is terrible! How can I read it! You never wrote so poorly before."

"That is the best I can do," I said in a feeling of utter helplessness. I felt for all the world as though I was breaking, going to pieces, losing my mind.

Around this time, I drew the conclusion: "I am losing my mind."

Then I resolved to make the greatest effort I could, to hold myself together, to save myself from going stark mad as others had gone.

"I will not let these cell-mates goaded on by the cruel, inhuman communists, ruin me. I will disregard them." I resolved and I begged God to help me.

So with this resolve, supported by all the effort I had, and a redoubling of my prayers, I faced the future.

In a few days, I felt I had gotten hold of myself, with God's help I had won. I had saved myself from going mad. The cell-mates said I no longer talked in my sleep. I was able to act, to decide and carry out my decisions.

I was saved.

·30·

General Tou Chengs

"I HOPE THAT son of a b—— is shot," said chu chang Tito to activist Wang one cold day in the winter of 1953, as these two worthies returned to the cell.

They had been called to attend a big tou cheng of four or five prisoners, in the prison "hall." The shouts of the tou chengers could be faintly heard in my cell. They sounded like heinous cries from some distant inferno.

Both Tito and Wang related to the rest of the cell-mates the details of the tou cheng. They were evidently proud and elated for having been called to participate in it. And of course the lesson of the tou cheng must be brought home to all prisoners especially the stubborn, unreformed ones. Each gave full details of the events: how the prisoners had been brought forth separately, accused, denounced, and ordered to confess.

Some confessed and were dismissed, without further punishment. Two failed in their confession and the zealous activists demanded that they be shot. Each was handcuffed and shackled and led away to solitary confinement.

The prison officer concluded by telling the activists that the government appreciated their zeal and would consider their requests to shoot these two stubborn prisoners.

Tito and Wang each emphatically repeated their hope that the "People's" government would shoot these two prisoners—unreformed, stubborn, reactionary prisoners.

The other cell-mates vied with one another in loudly voicing their agreement with Tito and Wang.

"Shoot them! Shoot them!" they shouted.

I remained silent, horrified at the thought that these two poor wretches were facing death at the hypocritical, cowardly request of their fellow prisoners!

"What is on your mind, Rigney?" Tito asked. "What do you think about this tou cheng? Do you agree with the rest of this cell that they should get shot or do you sympathize with them?"

"Yes, I feel sorry for them," I said, unable to hide my sympathy, "I do not like to have any prisoner shot. I hope the government will not shoot them."

"That only shows, Rigney, how reactionary, unreformed you are! You will be among the next to be so tou changed, I can assure you, and I hope the government shoots you!" Tito shouted.

For weeks Tito repeatedly predicted that I would be publicly tou changed.

The prison authorities, he said, were preparing for more such tou chengs for such prisoners as me.

Then one day I was called out and lined up with a few prisoners of other cells. I was resigned to a public tou chenging with the activists, including Tito and Wang, who accompanied me, demanding that I be shot.

It seems that there just is no end to the kinds of tortures to which the Chinese communists submit their prisoners.

We were marched over to the "hall," a big room, with the bare ground as the floor. Some one hundred prisoners were present.

A name was called out. A frightened, pale prisoner arose or was forced to arise and in a daze, made his way to the front.

It seemed all hell broke loose. Most of the hundred prisoners sitting on the ground burst forth in screams and howls, cursing, abusing the poor wretch, who was forced to stand with his head down.

Ever so often, an exceptionally zealous activist, throwing all shame and self-respect to the winds, arose, rushed up to the accused victim, waving his fist in his face and shouting, "Ti tou! (Down with your head!)," seized his head and jerked it down.

The accused made several efforts to confess but the crowd shouted him out. Sometimes a large part of the crowd jumped to their feet crowding around him, carrying on like so many mad men.

At last, after about an hour of this, the officer stepped forward, put handcuffs and fetters on the accused, and led him away.

Then a second name was called and a rather short-sized, frightened man of refined features arose and walked before the howling mob. He went through quite the same ordeal as the first.

Wang at the end shouted to shoot him, and several times rose to his feet shaking his fist, yelling accusations and curses.

This prisoner was also put in chains and led away.

On returning to our cell, Wang said that the second accused was Wu, his brother-in-law. Wang was hoarse from his shouting at his own brother-in-law, shouting even for his execution.

I had refrained from all this shouting and as a consequence was subjected to much questioning by Tito. At the end I had to write a paper, expressing all my thoughts about these awful ordeals.

I wrote that I did not like them and felt sorry for the accused.

A year later, similar tou chengs were held again. This time Wu who had suffered eight months in handcuffs and fetters was among the mob and to my disgust was one of the most zealous activists accusing, cursing the two victims.

Again I was obliged to explain why I had showed such sympathy and lack of interest in these tou chengs.

I wrote in detail about how I felt sorry for the accused and how hypocritical I thought the other prisoners acted in accusing the two victims.

I wrote that Our Blessed Lord must have dealt with just such a scene when he came on the woman who had been taken in adultery, being accused and about to be stoned to death, and how he wrote on the sand, "Let him without sin throw the first stone."

But I thought that these two victims for whom I had so much sympathy in a few weeks would be activists like Wu, accusing others.

So the folly went on in Ts'ao Lan Tzu.

·31·

Germ Warfare

As FAR as I can remember it was in the spring of 1952, that I first learned of the charges made by the Chinese communists that the Americans were conducting germ warfare in Korea.

I learned that there was something in the air from the cartoons in the papers that were sent around for reading. In many cartoons, rats, notorious carriers of disease, were depicted, being introduced, in one way or the other, into Korea, by the Americans.

From these cartoons I deduced that the communist government was using characteristically dirty tactics to cover up severe losses their armies were suffering in Korea from epidemics by accusing the American Armed Forces of conducting germ warfare.

The communist papers were full of articles bearing these accusations and many study periods in prison were spent discussing these articles of the local Peking press.

Then the confession of an American Air Force flyer was published in English and Chinese by the communist press. But this contained no conclusive evidence of such warfare. The flyer stated that he had dropped dud bombs, which I concluded could have been other than germ bombs.

A certain foreign Protestant minister made an investigation in China and Korea of the evidence advanced by the Chinese to prove the germ warfare of the Americans in Korea. He concluded that the accusations of the Chinese communists were true: the U. S. Armed Forces had employed germ warfare in

Korea. He based his conclusion in part on the corroborative testimony of many Chinese ministers of religion whom he had interviewed in communist China on this matter and who concurred with the communist government in accusing the Americans of germ warfare.

This foreigner demonstrated his unreliableness when he accepted the testimony of the Chinese ministers who were not free to question the communist papers, to frankly express their sincere opinions, to say otherwise than they actually did.

I considered the doings of this individual clergyman shameful.

Later, an international scientific commission came to China and Korea and investigated the germ warfare case. They concluded that the U. S. Armed Forces had employed germ warfare.

This conclusion and further confessions of American flyers shot down by the communists in Korea led me to believe that the Americans had conducted a test of germ bombs.

I suffered much persecution over this case, since I refused to believe that the Americans were conducting full scale germ warfare.

Then, I was declared to be the source of all the vermin: lice, fleas, etc., of the cells in which I was imprisoned, and treated accordingly by many cell-mates. Some of these scowled at me when they found vermin on their clothes or bed rolls. Others shunned me as particularly infested with lice or were very loud in their demands that I inspect my clothes for lice.

When I read in a communist English publication an accusation that the U. S. Government had "shamelessly endeavored to hide their crimes" against humanity by denying that the American Armed Forces in Korea had ever resorted to germ warfare, I was delighted and accepted this statement of Washington as true.

The communists then published confessions of some 21 American flyers, in which it was stated that they had dropped germ bombs.

These confessions agreed on some important points. But this did not convince me since I knew the dirty tactics of the Chinese communists that resort not only to tortures and cajolery to force or induce prisoners to confess what they suggest or demand them to confess but actually change, delete or insert parts of a text of a confession to suit their plans.

I could not believe that these flyers were traitors or cowards.

I had served as a chaplain in the U. S. Army Air Force in the Second World War and knew that combat flyers are not traitors or cowards.

The U. S. Marines certainly have demonstrated outstanding valor and loyalty, and Marine Officers command my highest respect.

"These flyers, Air Force and Marine, are not cowards," I thought. "If they have made false confessions, something happened to them. They were tricked, or tortured by subtle, refined tortures, quite new even in the world of perversion and cruelty, until they were no longer their old selves and confessed."

The communist papers claimed that these flyers were to be court-martialed on their return to the U. S. A.

I hoped the American government would not punish these airmen who had offered their lives in the service of their country, and had failed to stand up against techniques they had never known of or for which they had never been prepared.

"If the American government punishes them," I thought, "they will be playing into the hands of the contemptible, fiendish communists who are trying to break the morale of the flyers, and to frighten the American youth from enlisting in the Air Force."

On my arrival in Hong Kong, I learned that the U. S. Armed Forces had set up training centers to prepare cadet airmen to face the cunning Chinese communist prison and court procedures.

I was pleased to learn of this.

Some Americans, shall I call them blind sentimentalists or communist sympathizers, were shocked at the so-called brutality of such a training.

Do such people, sitting so cozily in their comfortable parlours, realize what threatens their liberties?

Do they oppose giving our brave youth who fight our battles all the protection and training we can?

Do they realize that communism employs new weapons, psychological weapons, and we must prepare our armed forces to withstand them?

They reply, "But if we train our youth to resist such and such techniques, our training is useless because the Reds will learn about it and change their techniques."

To this I say, "Why do the Reds learn of this? Who has informed the Reds one way or the other? How can such individuals be controlled?" The problem then shifts to one of security.

Something new happened in the East Court of Ts'ao Lan Tzu, in the early spring of 1954.

All the prisoners were called out one morning and informed of the new exercise program, in which all, who were able, were to participate. As far as I remember, there were about one hundred prisoners in that court when the exercise program was initiated. Later, by June, the number had dropped to about 50.

Every morning we gathered in the courtyard for group running followed by calisthenics that together lasted about twenty minutes.

Previous to this the only exercise was two daily trips to the latrine of the courtyard, or a trip to the court of the judge.

The rest of the twenty four hours were spent in unsunned, damp cells.

Rheumatism was common. I suffered from pains in my joints which I think were due either to rheumatism or vitamin deficiencies or both.

Because of the stiffness of my joints and the rheumatic-like pains I suffered, the running exercise, done in formation style to the speed of the leader, as well as the calisthenics, were painful.

Since these physical exertions were painful, I performed them in a clumsy or imperfect manner, which invited persecution.

I was cursed by the leader, a young squirt of a prisoner, for not performing the calisthenics to his liking. The cellmates, especially Julian, often created great scenes, because I was too slow, or stiff in the bending exercise.

Frequently, in the cell I was obliged to practice the calisthenics under the supervision of the cell-mates.

Consequently even physical exercises were made occasions of persecutions, mild in themselves, but many of these mild persecutions in their accumulative effect, over a long space of time, became grave, serious and big.

·32·

A Long Sentence in the Making

THE SPRING of 1954 came and with it renewed hopes that the Kind Master, Whom I served the best I could, at the intercession of His Blessed Mother and His Foster Father would give me more strength to unite closer with Him in carrying His cross and doing His holy will, and perhaps even obtain my release.

From the beginning of my imprisonment I told Our Blessed Lord that I could no longer be united with Him as a priest since the communists forbade and rendered me unable to celebrate the Holy Sacrifice of the Mass. I then told Him I could only be united with Him as a victim, but prayed for the grace to be a better victim.

In the early months of my imprisonment I prayed earnestly for my release. As time went on, I prayed more for strength to bear up, to become more and more Christ-like, and less for my release.

Around the end of May, I was moved back to the West compound to section A or the southern section.

It was a relief to get away from the cell where Teng and his two successors, who were not much better, had held sway.

Soon after my transfer to the West compound, I was called to court. My regular judge presided. He asked me how I was getting on, how I spent the past year, what I had been thinking about and the like.

I do not remember what I told him beyond the fact that I had been admitted to the study group around the preceeding

April but could not follow the discussions or readings from the paper because of my ignorance of Chinese.

"To what U. S. government organization do you belong?" he said.

"I belong to no U. S. government organization," I said, not a little surprised with this question. "I thought," I continued, "I had made this clear before."

He questioned me further on this point but I remained firm.

"How does the U. S. government control the American S.V.D. (Divine Word Missionaries)?" he said.

"The U. S. government does not control the American S.V.D."

"It does and we know all about it. I am asking you only to see how honest you are."

"It is 36 years since I joined the American S.V.D. and I have always been in close contact with them. I know nothing of the U. S. government controlling them. Moreover, I personally do not believe that the U. S. government controls the American S.V.D."

"You want to sacrifice yourself for the American S.V.D.? You are willing to suffer for them? Alright, go ahead, you will suffer plenty for them.

"You have been in the S.V.D. so long and in America so long that you are unable to expose these two. You will pay for this.

"Did you ever hear of the U. S. Marine, Colonel Schwable?"

"Yes," I replied.

"Did you hear or read that he made important exposures of the U. S. Armed Forces, in Korea?"

"I have read about this in English publications of the 'People's' government."

"Now, Rigney, if you would make similarly big exposures of the U. S. government's control of the American S.V.D., you would receive a big reduction in your sentence. The 'People's' government will not shoot or electrocute you as the cruel American government electrocutes spies as they murdered the innocent Rosenbergs, but the 'People's' government will give you a long sentence. It is up to you to help yourself by helping the government and winning a reduction in your sentence."

"I have told you the truth, I know of no U. S. control of the American S.V.D. To say otherwise would be confessing falsely and I have had enough of that. I will not make a false confession.

"What!" he roared as he pounded his desk, "Are you threatening the 'People's' government?"

"No, I am just telling the truth."

After this session, I felt relieved in one way since this was the first time in three years that I was told by the court I would not get shot. On the other hand I was depressed with the prospects of a long, bitter prison sentence.

During this period I had several court sessions. In one of them the judge waved a pile of papers in the air and said: "On the evidence presented by Mark (whom he named, and I knew) the 'People's' government can give you a life sentence."

I stood motionless and made no reply.

"Look, here is Mark's signature!" and he presented the confession so I could see the signature made below the confession done in Chinese.

"This is one good confession Mark made," the judge said.

As I knew Mark, I was sure he had been cajoled or forced into some melodramatic and false confession about me, as I later told the chu chang so he could report to the court my reactions to this.

The judge also told me in those days, "If you do not confess about the U. S. government control of the American S.V.D., your case will not be reviewed every year as in the past but only every three years."

This meant that I could have an opportunity to win a court reduction in sentence only every three years. This was not good news.

The judge also maintained that the U. S. government controlled the Roman S.V.D. and the Catholic Church.

I denied both of these.

Later he said that if the Roman S.V.D. and the Catholic Church follow the same policy towards communism as the American government does, then the American government controls them.

"If that is what you call control," I said, "then the U. S. government does control them."

He then pressed me to state facts to support this, but I gave none in spite of this pressing, shouting and pounding on his desk. Consequently my bare agreement unsupported by plausible facts meant nothing. The absence of facts removed the grounds to support the admission of control.

My confession of July 1953, was given me to rewrite, reducing it to about fifteen pages. This impressed me as a good sign and in spite of all the judge had threatened about a life or long sentence, I thought that perhaps this was a preparation to release me. I rewrote it several times, finally producing a 20-page confession. The judge made substantial changes, adding, deleting or changing words. Thus I had written that a Divine Word priest friend of mine could have known an F.B.I. agent among his many friends and acquaintances. The judge changed the "could have known an F.B.I. agent" to "had known an F.B.I. agent."

I wrote, "as rector of Fu Jen, I gave intelligence—" He changed this to "under the cloak of a priest I gave intelligence —" I objected to this change but the judge stated that "when a priest gives intelligence, he gives it under the cloak of a priest." On the basis of this explanation I let it go, hoping to be released to explain or correct all these distorted statements if they were ever published.

One day I was called to the court and told I would have to record my confession on a wire recorder. To hesitate, I thought, would jeopardize my chance of getting released, so I did not argue or hesitate. I also thought that the recording was being made for presenting in a higher court.

Later, I thought the recording might be broadcasted over Radio Peking, and the written confession published, while I was held in prison where I could make no explanations. This weighed on me for about a year.

Letters From Home

IN THE NEW CELL, however, the same brain-washing and pressing prisoners to confess and accuse others continued.

Many Catholics, including priests and brothers were arrested that summer of 1954. They were dealt with harsher than the other prisoners. I remember one brother, who was cruelly beaten by the acting chu chang, Judas, a "progressive Catholic," who was a tall, well built six-footer. The brother, a brave and stouthearted Chinese, took these tortures with outstanding fortitude. Several times Judas, in a fit of uncontrollable rage, seized the chain of the brother's fetters and with all his might, jerked them up and down: the sharp edges of the rusty iron fetter bands dealt painful blows on the sensitive bones of the shins and feet, causing bruises and drawing blood.

The brother in agony stretched out his legs, clinched his jaws, bearing the pain.

On one occasion, I seized the arm of Judas crying, "Stop, you will break his bones. You are not allowed to beat prisoners." He stopped but what he reported about me to the prison officer, I never heard. It undoubtedly contributed to my further detention and sentence in prison, while most of the other foreign priests were released in the spring and summer of that year of 1954. Such actions as I had done were dangerous and usually brought punishment for both the doer and the one protected or defended.

In 1952, beating of prisoners was forbidden by the prison,

but it seemed the officials granted many exceptions since this brother was beaten many times. On one occasion, Judas stamped on the brother's feet so hard that I thought he broke the bones of the poor brother's foot arch.

Judas defended the Ke Hsing Huei (pro-Communist Reformation Committee consisting of a few renegade Catholics collaborating with the Red government) of the Pei Tang (North Church or Cathedral) of Peking and tried without success to induce the brother to support it.

Later a prisoner, Brutus, came to our cell to conduct the tou cheng-ing and breaking down of the brother. On several occasions Brutus beat up the brother, dealing him hard blows in the face. The other cell-mates, excepting me, joined in the beating. Judas told them if they did not beat the brother, they were not on the side of the communist government.

To stand by and witness such brutality and tou cheng-ing hour after hour, day after day, dealt out to a helpless prisoner, was always a mental torture for me. And I witnessed such for over four years.

Judas was accustomed to hum Catholic hymns and parts of a mass in my hearing. I showed no reaction. Judas had shown his colors and I was on my guard against his provocations.

Had I joined his humming, or led off on a religious discussion, he could, and certainly would, have immediately reported me as spreading subversive propaganda, trying by means of religious appeals to wean "progressive Catholics" from the bosom of the government, etc.

Shortly after, the brother was moved to another cell and a young Chinese priest was brought in.

Judas and the other cell-mates pressed him as they had pressed the brother to support the Ke Hsing Huei.

To strengthen this brave young priest and to clarify before the "People's" government my stand, I asked a prisoner to translate for me to this young priest. "Is the Ke Hsing Huei united to the Bishop of Rome, the Pope?" I asked.

"No."

"Then since the government guarantees freedom of religion in China, we Catholics are free to support or not support the Ke Hsing Huei. To support the Ke Hsing Huei would be separating from communion with the Pope and this would be denying our Catholic religion since union with the Pope is essential to Catholicism. Therefore, we Catholics are not bound to support the Ke Hsing Huei. For my part, I do not support the Ke Hsing Huei. I am a Catholic and am resolved to remain a Catholic. If I supported this committee, I would be changing my religion. The government declares I am free to select my religion, and I choose to be and remain a Catholic."

A few days after this, I was sentenced.

In mid September, 1954, I was given five letters, air mailed from the States in June, that had been sent by my brother and four sisters through the Chinese Red Cross. These were the first letters I had received from my relatives since my arrest in July, 1951. I was simply delighted with them and read them over and over. I kept them in a convenient place so I could get to them. I would have read them more frequently but feared that such would only draw the wrath of the cell-mates and officers for showing too much interest in family affairs instead of the "great absorbing" questions of communism, marxism, socialism, the socialization of China.

The judge gave me permission to answer these letters which I did, writing about the family and friends, with one sentence about myself: "My health is good and I am well cared for." To write about being in prison, or prison experiences or life in China would have been criminal and punished and I would not degrade myself by obsequiously extolling the "People's"

China, although such would have pleased the communists and won favors from them.

I also had asked the judge for permission to write to my relatives for some money since I had only 56,000 Jen Min Chuan or equivalent to about $2.80 in U. S. money. I feared too that if war were declared between the U. S. and communist China, I would be in a tough position with no money to purchase shou chih (toilet paper), soap and the like. Then my teeth were in very poor shape. I suffered daily from them. "If I had more money," I thought, "I could perhaps get proper dental treatment." Moreover, I did not know how long I would be in prison.

The judge granted this request and I wrote asking my brother the Rev. Dr. J. Francis Rigney, Professor of History at San Diego University, for a little money.

·34·

Sentenced

"You are sentenced to ten years of imprisonment," the interpreter said for the judge.

On September 21, 1954, the officer made me pack my belongings. Coming at this time, I thought I might be released.
I was nervous as I packed.
The guard then led me to a side room where I was told to open all my bundles for inspection.
I was not nervous, I was excited.
"At last," I thought, "I am going to be released."
I began to plan what I would do after my release.
I would call on the good S. Sp. S. (Holy Ghost Missionary Sisters) and thank them from the bottom of my heart for all they had done for me, in prison.
They lived near the prison, about one English mile, or a little over one and one-half kilometers, at Nan Wei Hutung San Hao, (Nan Wei Lane, No. 3) Tai Ping Ts'ang.
I would inquire from them whether there were any of my confreres, Divine Word Missionaries, left in Peking and if so where they lived.
I pictured my meeting with these confreres. There was so much to ask them. How they were? Had any been arrested? Had any been deported?
My first mass after being released! How I longed for this! I had dreamed so often of celebrating mass. Now it was soon to be a reality—but I was not entirely sure.

After this inspection, in which all my notes made in my efforts to learn Chinese, were destroyed, I was led by an officer to a room in a courtyard west of the court rooms in which I had had most of my sessions. Before entering this room I met my usual interpreter. She said, "You are going to receive your sentence."

At this I was more nervous.

I expected to be released by court order. "Perhaps," I thought, "I will first be sentenced, then a second order will be pronounced reducing my term to the time already spent in prison. This would entail my immediate release or discharge."

I entered the court room with the interpreter. The judge was waiting. We three were the only ones in the room.

"You are now to be sentenced," the interpreter said.

I stood at attention, while the judge, whom I could not remember ever having seen before, read my sentence. He read only one document.

The interpreter followed, giving me an interpretation.

As far as I can remember the sentence stated that—I had been sent to China by the U. S. government to take over German influence in China; collected and reported economic, military, political, educational, and social intelligence to the U. S. consulate and U. S. espionage agencies as well as to other imperialistic consulates and embassies and negotiating missions, such as the British, Dutch, Belgium, French and Italian, before and after "liberation"; opposed and sabotaged the progressive movement in China, as well as the reformation of Fu Jen University and the religious reformation policy of the "People's" government.

"For these crimes," the interpreter concluded, "you are sentenced to ten years imprisonment."

I was shocked indeed!

I was not released but on the contrary, sentenced to ten long years.

"Still it could have been worse, 15, 20, or more years," I thought.

"Do you have anything to say?" the judge asked.

"I have nothing to say," I said.

For a year or so I had prepared this statement, should I be given a long sentence. I had resolved not to fall on my knees admitting my "crimes," thanking the generous "People's" government and begging mercy.

The judge seemed a little upset by this noncommittal answer.

"But you are a spy, are you not?"

At this, I thought that I would have to continue admitting that I was a spy according to the communist definition. To do otherwise would only bring me into more trouble.

"Yes," I replied.

"I am going to send you to a prison factory where you can work out your reformation by labor. I want you to work well."

"I will do my best."

The judge did not tell me when the sentence began. I was of the opinion, which was later verified, that it began on the day of my arrest, 25th of July, 1951, and would last until July 25th, 1961.

In bewilderment, I left the court room to find the prison officers opening my bundles again for the second search. More articles were lost, destroyed or confiscated.

The interpreter returned the articles taken from me on the day of my arrest. The watch and automatic pencil were damaged. They had been crushed while being kept by the prison authorities. No apology was offered. No effort was made to repair these articles damaged as a result of the neglect or carelessness of the officials.

I did not complain. "What is this compared to all we S.V.D. fathers have so far lost—Fu Jen University, S.V.D. properties, including the seminary; to mention only two?" I thought. After this I was ordered into a jeep—an American jeep—and my right wrist, handcuffed to that of another prisoner, a Japanese, who was being taken with me.

We then drove down to the southwest corner of the southern or Chinese city to the Jen Min Fa Yuan Chien Yu, Hsuan Men Wei, Tzu Hsing Lu, (The People's Court Prison, outside Hsuan gate, Tzu Hsing street.)

The drive was about four English miles or six and a half kilometers.

This was my first time outside the walls of Ts'ao Lan Tzu since my arrest on July 25, 1951, a space of three years and two months.

I was most impressed by the somber, depressed expressions on the faces of the people of all ages and both sexes, that I saw on this journey.

"These are not the 'Peking' people I knew," I thought, "They are habitually gay or smiling. Now they look so sober. I understand. They are under the cloud of communism. The red star of Mao Tse-tung was an illusion. It turned out to be a cloud."

These faces told me more than books could about the real effect of communism on the Peking people.

We arrived at the prison. There were high walls, with higher towers manned by armed guards at the corners. The walls were newly built. The communists had enlarged the Kuomingtang prison to meet the demand for more prison space. Everywhere, in the Peking area, inside and outside the walled cities, are new prisons. Many are requisitioned or confiscated residences. The Chinese police state is a Chinese prison state. And yet the Chinese are forced to sing songs that China was never so free!

I was in the prison factory, on Tzu Hsing Lu, under a ten year prison sentence.

A Match Box Maker

NEAR THE entrance of the prison factory on Tzu Hsing Lu, my bundles were again laid open and examined for the third time. A few more articles of mine were lost. The wind blew away much of my valuable shou chih (toilet paper). The officials took in keeping my penknife, the little money I had left which was about 56,000 Jen Ming Chuan or equivalent to about $2.80 in U. S. money.

This was the remnant of the 400,000 Jen Ming Chuan I had on me when arrested plus the 1,000,000 J.M.C. found in my living quarters at Li Kwang Chiao Nan Chieh, I Hao (Fu Jen) when the Sepo searched those quarters after my arrest.

Each Divine Word Missionary at Fu Jen had been issued 1,000,000 Jen Ming Chuan, equivalent to a little less than $50.00 U. S. money. We were to keep this money for an emergency, as arrest.

The officials did not take my rosary which I prized as my most valuable belonging. It had been given to me by my former superior, Most Reverend Adolph A. Noser, S.V.D., the former Bishop of Accra, Gold Coast, British West Africa, and present Bishop of Alexishaven, New Guinea. I valued this rosary especially as a memory of this self sacrificing bishop, whose spirituality has ever been a model to me.

After this searching and registration at the entrance, we prisoners were ordered to carry our bundles to the top floor of the three storied building, recently built by the communists.

Here my bundles were searched for the fourth time, with more losses.

After the usual confusion of the Chinese communists, I was ordered down to the second floor to Section 1, Ward 1, where my bundles were again hastily opened and their diminishing contents thrown over the dirty floor of the prison for another and fifth search. This time I lost my Chinese shoes, and face rag. Many other articles lost for the time being were recovered months later, in the heaps of held-over belongings of prisoners.

My rosary was taken away, as well as the few photos of some of my relatives which I had received a few days previous in the letters finally allowed to be sent me by my relatives through the Chinese Red Cross.

After this inspection, I was assigned to Cell No. 1. The number of my living quarter was Section No. 1, Ward No. 1, Cell No. 1, or 111.

There were 25 prisoners in cell 111. There were eight cells in this ward, and each cell held about 25 prisoners, making an average of about 200 in the ward.

The cell was about 16 feet wide, to the right and left of the door, and about 12 feet deep. Opposite the door were two large windows each about 3 feet wide and six feet high. On either side of the 4-foot aisle were wooden kangs or beds about 12 feet by 6 feet. There was a single 15 candle power electric light in the center of the ceiling.

The kangs were used for sleeping, for eating, for studying and for working. The movable boards were taken up after a night's rest and arranged to serve as benches for factory work and then rearranged to serve as dinner tables. In study periods, the dinner, or night arrangement of the kangs was used.

Twice a day, about 15 to 30 minutes after rising and in the afternoon about 4 o'clock, all the prisoners of the ward left their cells, formed a double line in the corridor, and filed down to the latrine.

There was a toilet in each ward that was far too small and so poorly built and equipped that flushing had to be supplemented by buckets of water, hand drawn and poured. This toilet could be visited for urination with permission of the cell leader or pen chang, and in emergencies for a bowel movement after asking permission from your own pen chang and usually a second pen chang in charge of the latrine permissions.

We ate three times a day. The meals were little better than at Ts'ao Lan Tzu. The wo tou and pai tsai were often supplemented by hsien tsai (or salted vegetable). In the autumn and early winter we received rice once a week. After Chinese New Year, in mid winter, we received rice only once a month. With rice went a soup with meat, usually 4 or 6 pieces of meat, the size and twice the thickness of an American quarter of a dollar.

The cell had two pen changs, or cell leaders, the head or first pen chang and the assistant or second.

It was difficult for me to adjust myself to the crowded conditions of the cell. We were always crowded. At night 8 or 9 slept on each kang, 4 slept in the aisle, at times one or two slept on boards placed each night from kang to kang at the window end of the aisle. The rest slept in the corridor. At meals, work, brainwashing and "recreation" all the inmates were corralled in this cell.

Movement about in the cell at all times, night or day, was difficult.

The head pen chang, Chu, was quite decent towards me, at first. A day or so later, apparently after he received instructions, he was a genuine "running dog" of his communist masters. I was one of the cell-mates who suffered under his constant persecution. I was suffering from rheumatic-like pains from the damp, under-heated cells, as well as I think, from deficiency in vitamins. Consequently it was painful for me to move fast. But Chu, every time he saw me, roared, "Rui Ko

Ni! Kuai! Kuai! (Rigney, hurry! hurry!)" He lost no opportunity to persecute me on other grounds.

There was an activist in the cell, a sort of third pen chang, who peered out through thick lensed spectacles. He reminded me, on first sight, of one of the depraved characters in a novel of Dickens and he subsequently lived up to this in his persecution of unprogressive cell-mates including myself.

This was a match box factory.

I became a match box maker.

My specialty was to assemble the rims of the tray part of the match box. I received a strip of paper with a flat strip of thin wood pasted on it. These had to be folded into a tray with the paper folded over the edges. This was then thrown to another worker who pasted a bottom on it.

This was light factory work, but all workers were obliged to work faster and faster.

In my specialty 2,000 trays a day were expected, 3,000 were considered fast, 4,000 and above, very fast.

I attained a record for myself of 4,200 in the end of April 1955. This was very fast but others were even faster.

The Chinese are experts at such work and seem to delight in it. They are experts at precision work and I often thought that if the Chinese ever turn to the manufacturing of watches, cameras, miscroscopes and the like, they will excel all producers of such precision instruments in the West.

·36·

My Last Friends: Chinese Holy
Ghost Missionary Sisters

I NEEDED some supplies as aprons, winter bedding, winter clothing, soap, a small stool to be used at work and to sit on at the many brainwashing talks and stage performances we were obliged to attend.

I asked for permission to write to the S. Sp. S. sisters who had so generously sent me supplies before. After about three weeks I was finally informed I could write to the sisters for what I needed in the line of supplies, but food was excepted.

Chu wrote a card to the sisters for me in Chinese, requesting the supplies I needed. I also asked them for a little money if they had it and could spare it. The request was made because I did not know if my brother in the U.S.A., whom I had requested for money, would be allowed to send me any.

In about two weeks more, the good Holy Ghost Missionary Sisters sent me my requested supplies, as well as 100,000 Jen Ming Chuan equivalent to about four U. S. dollars. All this, including the money, was a great help. With the money, I could purchase a little extra food each week, as eggs, sugar and occasionally a little wheat bread.

These good sisters, without my asking them, sent me the same amount of money on three subsequent occasions.

In prison, I thought that the "People's" government must allow them to receive money from my society for me through Switzerland. Later in September, 1955, on reaching Hong

Kong, I learned that no money was sent them from outside China, that these good Chinese sisters worked with their own hands to earn money to supply me with the needs I had in prison! They also supplied other prisoners! When I learned this, I was deeply moved and have not yet found words to express my esteem and gratitude to them.

Chu, the pen chang, improved his attitude and behavior towards me around the beginning of December. I took this as a good sign. I had developed the idea by this time that a prisoner could gauge his standing with the government by the way the cell leader treated him. Hence, when Chu began to be decent, I thought that the government was becoming favorably disposed towards me.

About this time, in the beginning of December 1954, I was called with Monsignor Martina and a Japanese, into one of the offices of the prison and asked to fill out a biographical statement. I thought that perhaps this was a step towards my release. Christmas was coming and the communists often release prisoners just before an important day. I thought that I might be released before this feast. As a matter of fact, Monsignor Martina was released within a couple of weeks and the Japanese was not to be seen about the time Monsignor Martina disappeared from the prison. But I was not released.

When I was not released by Christmas and Chu began to be nasty towards me again, in January 1955, I concluded that my standing with the government had deteriorated.

Throughout my stay in the prison factory, I suffered from frequent, severe head and chest colds, frequent attacks of diarrhea, toothaches and rheumatism. The colds were due, I think, to the under-heated, damp, cells. The diarrhea I traced to the unsanitary policy of using only cold water, with no soap to wash our pai tsai bowls and chop sticks, both of which were used promiscuously. My teeth had been bothering me since the spring of 1952. My gums were swollen and painful, a beriberi condition due to vitamin deficiency. The rheumatic-like pains were due, I think, to the cold, damp cells and, I think, to vitamin deficiency.

I often went to the prison physicians. This was quite an experience. A sick prisoner notified the pen chang who in turn notified the medical officer through a special pen chang. In the late morning, the names of all the sick applicants were shouted in the corridor. The sick then lined up and were marched upstairs to a big open room where four physicians sat at a table. The sick were queued up by shouting pen changs, for each doctor. There was no privacy. There were no adequate consultations. In my case with my poor Chinese, it was impossible to explain my complaints. The doctors, all prisoners, did the best they could in the limited time at their disposal and the wretched clinical conditions. Their medicament supplies were evidently insufficient.

Later, in the spring, the physicians held consultations in cells set aside and equipped for clinical work, but even here there was little privacy and little time for proper consultation.

All the prisoners were vaccinated and received anti-typhoid injections in good order, considering the large number of prisoners, some 4,000 or 5,000 in all, as I estimated them at full indoctrination gatherings.

In February, I was called into the pai chang's or warden's office. The warden showed me a box of food and medicine my brother had sent me through the International Red Cross of Geneva, Switzerland. This left Geneva on January 7, 1955.

I had to itemize all the articles of the box and sign that I had received them. Then they were all taken away, to be kept for me.

In April, I was very sick with diarrhea, nausea and a severe chest cold. Several times I felt like vomiting. At last in the evening, I could stand the nausea no longer and asked for permission to go to the latrine. Here I vomited first food, then a quantity, a half a pint or more, of blood. The blood shocked me.

On returning to my cell, I sat quietly and tried to explain the blood. I ruled out a lung hemorrhage because I had noticed no blood in my sputum. I thought that most probably it was due to a stomach ulcer or infection, as dysentery.

I reported this vomiting of blood to the pen chang and had a consultation with a physician the next morning. The doctor examined my chest with a stethoscope and then prescribed tablets to be taken every four hours for 24 hours. I think the tablets were sulfa drugs. They made me sick. I was also excused from work and allowed to sit up in the cell but not permitted to lie down although I felt very sick. Special food—rice—was given me for a few days but I had no appetite and ate very little. I was not troubled any more with vomiting of blood.

I wrote a request to the prison authorities, asking them to give me the food and medicine package my brother had sent me, since it contained ovalmaltine, which I could use to the benefit of my health. My request passed unheeded!

·37·

The Skies are the Same

"How LOVELY are the skies," I thought, as we filed out of the
prison factory building at dawn, into the open ground, which
was some 300 feet square, on our way to the latrine.

It was so restful to raise my head and look up into the clear,
blue skies of Peking.

The sordid prison was so different from the free world that
I had known in China, in America, in Europe and in Africa!
The cruel, devilish communists who built the sordid prison
and tortured all in China to force them to accept an unnatural
system of Godlessness was so different from the rest of the
world where the deepest, most ardent aspirations of man
found expression!

The damnable, cruel prison with its subtle and brutal tortures, its hypocritical, fiendish, inhuman communist authorities was so different from the rest of the cultured, Christian
world that I knew!

But the skies, the beautiful, blue skies were the same in or
out of Tzu Hsing Lu Prison!

To raise my head and look at the skies, the boundless ex-
panse of space, lifted me above the duplicity and injustice of
communist China into a realm that Mao Tse-tung and Chou
En-lai and the rest of the communist gangsters knew nothing
about.

"Our Blessed Lord ascended into those skies, Constantine
the Great saw a Cross with the words: 'In hoc signo vinces. (In
this sign thou shalt conquer)' in them," I often thought, "and
somewhere beyond are the eternal realms of heaven, where

as the Blessed Paul wrote we shall see God not as 'now through a mirror in an obscure manner, but then face to face (I Cor. XIII, 12),' and again 'Eye has not seen, nor ear heard, neither hath it entered into the heart of man, what things God hath prepared for them that love Him. (I Cor. II, 9).'"

And at night when we were forced to attend those cheap, Chinese communist propaganda or half-baked Russian films, it was a relief to look above the wretched cinema screen to the star spangled heavens!

The stars were the same in Tzu Hsing Lu as in the free world!

I recognized the constellations Orion, Cygnus, the brilliant Pleiades, Ursa Major or the Big Dipper, Ursa Minor with its North Star, and the like, that I had known from boyhood. They were the same beautiful groups of stars that I had learned to know over forty years ago in Chicago, on the other side of the earth.

Yes, the communists may come and go, but the stars remain forever!

There were other scenes I remember from those open grounds—the poor wretch of a blind prisoner, with his empty eye sockets,—in handcuffs and fetters.

I often wondered, what on earth could he have done of a criminal nature!

I remember the aged, the crippled, the lame, wobbling out to the latrine! One day I counted 15 crippled prisoners out of a line of 150. That was 10%. I thought the communists must have a special hatred for the aged, the infirm, the disabled, the crippled, the blind.

These unfortunates are unproductive and therefore have little welcome in a marxist set up.

I had always considered slave labor as the cheapest of labor. I had read about slaves and their labor in the U.S.A. before the

American Civil War. I had seen slaves working in the Arabian and Moorish world of North Africa, especially in the Sahara Desert of Mauritania, French Africa.

But in communist China I discovered that there is one type of labor lower, cheaper than slave labor and that is communist Chinese prison labor.

A slave is fed and clothed by his master.

Not so the average laborer in the dank prison factory of communist China.

The prisoners, with exceptions, in the prison factories of the quisling Mao Tse-tung, are clothed, and partly fed by their relatives.

The shameless Chinese communists do not even clothe, properly feed, provide bedding, toilet paper, or soap for most of their countless millions of prisoners, most of whom are thrown into prison on trumped-up, unjust charges.

These prisoners are cruelly and unjustly forced to serve long sentences of 5, 10, 15, 20, 30 years or life, during which they labor in state prison factories, producing match boxes, bricks, thread, cloth, etc., or on state farms.

The police state of communist China is largely based on the economy of the prison state—an economy lower than slave economy!

·38·

4,200 Match Boxes in One Day

AROUND the beginning of April 1955, I was changed from Cell No. 1 to No. 3. My prison residence was 113, Section No. 1, Ward No. 1, Cell No. 3.

In this new cell, I was treated as never before. The pen chang or cell leader was the most considerate I had ever had. The assistant pen chang was likewise considerate and decent. The rest of the cell-mates, following the lead of the two pen changs, were also considerate. They did not treat me as well as they treated their Chinese fellow prisoners. This was to be expected. After all, I was an American, a Catholic priest. If Chinese prisoners in the communist prison of Tzu Hsing Lu would have treated me as well as they treated Chinese prisoners, they would have been inviting punishment from the communists. But the cell-mates treated me better than any other group of cell-mates I had ever had.

Moreover, I was given better working facilities.

Often I noticed that certain prisoners, who were actually fast and efficient or else were advanced in their progressive thinking, were given better facilities to work than other prisoners. They were appointed to work in places where there was relatively good light; where they had more room, elbow room, to enable them to work fast; they were provided with ample supplies and were given fast follow-up workers, who kept their products from accumulating to the point of piling up and being in the way.

I was given better working facilities.

"Well! well!" I thought, "these are good indications! The pen changs are decent, the cell-mates are decent, facilities for work have improved for me. These are good signs. The wind is blowing in the right direction. Whither it will blow me, is uncertain. So often in the past my hopes for release or deportation were raised only to meet with disappointment. These are improvements that indicate a more favourable attitude of the government towards me. Perhaps the government is considering or preparing to release or deport me. I must do my part so they can release me without losing face. They would not release me if they lost face in doing so. I have not and will not become communistic or "progressive" in my thinking, hence, there is only one way for me to help myself and that is by working well."

When the pen chang asked me in those days what I was thinking about, I told him, "I do not understand the newspaper or discussion classes," and I then added as emphatically as I could in my best Chinese embellished by pantomime, "I am working as well as I can and I want to improve my work to turn out more match boxes and better match boxes in order to have my sentence cut in half." The end of this statement was elucidated by cutting the air with my right hand, below my uplifted left hand as though I were cutting a suspended sausage by one blow.

Working under relatively favorable labor conditions and employing a technique I had hit upon around March 21, my output of match boxes increased.

A contest or movement to increase our production was started around the beginning of April 1955. The chiefs of the prison formally announced the contest to all the prisoners gathered in the open grounds, sitting on their little stools or bundles of clothes if they had either of these.

Two or three long speeches were given, lasting in all some two hours.

I sat through all this, as I had sat through so many similar

kai huai or meetings as well as stage productions, not understanding more than "Kai tsao! Kai tsao! Kai tsao! (Reform!
Reform! Reform!)" repeated umpteen times. I usually stead-
ied my head in my hands, my elbows resting on my knees, and
if no officers were around or it was night, I would pull my cap
well over my forehead and go off to sleep. Sometimes an activist would give me a poke in the side to awake me.

The day after this kai huai, the warden officer called all the
inmates of our ward out to the corridor, where we had to
listen to his motivation talk, peppered with "Kai tsao! Kai
tsao! Kai tsao!" for up to an hour.

This was followed by a pep talk by the pen chang or cell
leader who gave us some more kai tsao.

Later a kai huai was held in the cell in which each prisoner
was obliged to pledge himself to increase his production and
state the amount he would do. Moreover, the daily hours of
work were increased from 8 to 8-and-a-half hours because
of the lengthening days.

I was able to turn out 2,500 boxes a day and pledged to increase this to 2,800. I was quite certain I could do more but
to pledge your maximum in the beginning of such a movement was bad tactics, I thought, since the movement would
last several weeks and each week you would be called upon
to pledge to increase your production over the last. It would
be better to reserve your maximum for the grand finale and
score credit for it, than reach it the first week and be unable
to improve upon it, giving the impression that you were not
interested in the movement.

So I reached my 2,800 target with merit.

This output was raised to 3,200, then 3,500, then to my
surprise to 3,800 and at last to 4,200 match boxes a day! These
increases won me commendations. To turn out 4,000 match
boxes a day was very fast. So I had made a name for myself. I
tried to increase this to 4,500, hoping eventually to reach
5,000, but I had reached my peak. I turned out 4,000 a few
times afterwards, but never my 4,200 again.

In the final report, the chu chang credited me with working very well, for overshooting my pledged 2,800 by doing 4,200.

In the first year at Ts'ao Lan Tzu, from July 1951, to the following summer of 1952, we prisoners had our hair cut and beard clipped once every two months. We were never shaved. This meant that a prisoner never looked respectable.

The barbers were fellow prisoners.

Later, our hair and beards were sheared every month.

In Tzu Hsing Lu, we received tonsorial attention every two weeks, when our heads and beards were shaved or clipped.

Most prisoners, including me, chose to be shaven.

My head and face felt like a billiard ball, for one day out of two weeks. Then in April 1955, I decided to grow a beard.

"Better a beard," I thought, "than going around with fuzz, for 13 or 14 days out of each half month." Then I considered I could experiment with a beard with little inconvenience.

Back in my days in the mission of Accra, Gold Coast, West Africa, where I was Catholic chaplain and master at Achimota College, I experimented with a small beard but without success.

After letting my full beard grow about two or three weeks in Africa, I shaved my cheeks, leaving the fuzzy mustache, and chin beard. I looked as though I had just dipped my head into a big pot of jam—there was a black circle around my mouth, with a dot in the middle, on my lower lip.

I started to grow this beard at the beginning of the summer vacation of Achimota. A month later at the end of the vacation, I said mass at Achimota.

As I was in a hurry, I did something unwise: I failed to prepare or read over beforehand the gospel of that Sunday, which was read before mass.

I noticed that the students were taken by surprise when they saw me, but my embarrassment reached a climax when I read the first sentence of the gospel: "And turning to his disciples he said, 'Blessed are the eyes that see what you see! For I say to you, many prophets and kings have desired to see what you see and they have not seen it. (Luke X, 23, 24)."

I returned to the mission and shaved off my fuzz.

The cell-mates, in Tzu Hsing Lu, urged me to shave off my sprouting beard that grew in all directions. But I refused and thought, "This is something you cannot do!"

·39·

Back to Ts'ao Lan Tzu

On june 10, 1955, most of Ward No. 1, I included, were told to pack up their belongings. We were lined up and marched out to the open grounds where our belongings were searched.

My photos, money and such articles as had been held back by the ward officer, were returned.

"Are we going to be released or sent to the prison farm or some other prison factory?" I thought.

Soon, whatever illusions I had of being released, were again painfully destroyed.

We were marched past the road leading to the entrance into the old part of the prison which had been built by the Japanese. We stopped before a large, single-storied building with five wings radiating in a semicircle from the central entrance or hall.

I was assigned to a cell about 24 feet by 12 feet in which some 33 prisoners were corralled.

We did not make match boxes. We studied (were brainwashed) about ten hours a day, and were told by the ward officer that we would be assigned to a prison factory such as the textile factory in this prison or to some other prison factory.

"Who wants to buy garlic?" the pan chang asked one day. Everyone who had money instantly raised his hand. I joined the garlic rush.

"How much garlic do you want, Rui Ko-Ni?" the pan chang asked.

"How is it sold?"

"Quarter of a catty, half a catty, as much as you like."

"Give me one catty (one pound)," I said, thinking that I had better get a good supply while it was possible. The opportunity may not present itself again. I had seldom eaten fresh garlic before but now I thought it would be a good condiment for the tasteless, heavy, unleavened wo tou. Most cell-mates were purchasing it, hence there could be no objection to the consequent bad breaths of the garlic eaters. Never had I bought these pungent, strong-scented bulbs before, and I had only a faint idea of how bulky a pound of them would be.

No one else ordered as much as I had.

What a surprise I got a few days later when the garlic was delivered to me. I counted 25 bulbs, each containing about 8 to 10 bulblets, giving a total of about 200 to 250 bulblets. At the rate of 2 bulblets at each meal or 6 per day, my stock would last about 35 to 40 days.

And so it did. The stock of my cell-mates was soon exhausted and I found myself the only garlic eater in this cell and in the subsequent cells to which I was moved.

Often I noticed envious glances from cell-mates who were evidently garlic starved, or disturbed glances from those whose olfactory nerves were normally developed.

"This is once," I thought, "when I can get one over on the cell-mates. I have suffered much at their hands; now they are suffering from me." I calmly and cold bloodedly ate my garlic, about six bulblets a day for about one month and a half. One bite of wo tou and then a nibble of garlic, another bite of wo tou and another nibble of garlic.

What an imperialist I still was after almost four years of re-education!

On June 17, 1955, seven prisoners, I included, from various cells were told to pack up our bundles. Two of us were westerners, five were mongoloids.

We were ordered back to the match box factory to the same

ward I had been in prior to June 10, 1955. I was settled in Cell No. 2.

Chu was pen chang, and a different pen chang was he; quite considerate towards me, the match box maker who had a record of 4,200 boxes in a day.

Soon Chu asked me what I thought was the reason for returning me to my old building, to my old ward.

"I do not know," I said, "there were seven of us returned, two foreigners and five Chinese."

"No, you were all foreigners, seven foreigners, two westerners and five orientals."

"Oh, is that so?"

"What do you make of that?"

"Perhaps there is a threat of war and the 'People's' government is taking security measures and rounding up all foreigners to eventually gather them in a special prison."

I also thought that perhaps we foreigners were to be deported but dared not reveal this thought for fear the communist would take stringent measures to remove it.

So I was back at my trade; making match boxes, trying as I told Chu to make as many match boxes and as good match boxes as I could to cut my sentence in half, and I made my usual stroke of my right hand through the air as though I were cutting a sausage in half with one stroke.

Then on July 13, 1955, I was told to pack up my belongings.

"Take your time," Chu said, "and collect all your belongings since you will find it difficult to recover anything left behind."

I was excited.

"I am going to be deported, most likely," I thought.

With my bundles prepared, I was led down to the entrance of the prison where my bundles were opened and searched. My money, pocket knife, etc., held at the entrance, were handed over to an officer accompanying me, who, I thought, would give me these articles on releasing me.

The food package my brother had sent me, by air mail,

through the International Red Cross of Geneva on January 7, 1955, and a large food package from my relatives, were also given to me.

"This is grand! I must be going to be released!" I thought.

Soon I was ordered in a jeep with my bundles.

Then I received a shock: the officer handcuffed me.

"My," I thought, "this is bad. Released prisoners are not handcuffed. Perhaps," I thought, to keep my hopes up, "I am going to a court to be released by court order and afterwards my chains will be released. Or can it really be that I am going to another prison, to the prison farm or to a special prison for foreigners!" Such thoughts ran through my mind.

The jeep was driven out of the prison, north through the Hsuan Men (Hsuan gate) where I saw the famous old Nan Tang, (South Church) founded by the great Jesuit missionary Matteo Ricci, S.J., in the early part of the XVII Century.

"We are not going to the railroad station for a train to the prison farm or a distant prison," I thought.

On we drove.

"We are not going to the supreme court building. We have gone too far north," I said to myself.

On we drove.

"Perhaps we are going to Fu Jen, to Li Kwang Chiao Nan Chieh, I Hao, where I was arrested. How different will my homecoming be from my departure, that day on which I was arrested, July 25, 1951," I thought.

On we drove.

Then we made a turn up a hutung, which I did not recognize and after proceeding about five hundred feet passed through a gate I had never seen, a newly constructed gate, judging from the fresh paint it had. We entered a large compound with many buildings.

I looked at the buildings. They looked familiar.

Suddenly I realized where I was.

I was stunned!

"Goodness me! I am back in Ts'ao Lan Tzu—the Peking hell!" I said to myself.

I thought of how prisoners who had been sentenced and sent to the prison farm or some labor prison had been recalled to Ts'ao Lan Tzu for renewed "education" and confessions, when new evidence had been found against them.

"Why have they brought me here? Am I in for more of the old tortures of Ts'ao Lan Tzu? Perhaps," I thought desperately, hoping, holding out to the end, "I will be taken to court here in Ts'ao Lan Tzu and be released."

The future was uncertain but I was back in Ts'ao Lan Tzu!

In bewilderment, my handcuffs were removed. I was ordered out of the jeep into a small room—the room where my belongings were inspected for the first time on 21 September, 1954, the day on which I had been sentenced to ten years of imprisonment.

I squatted on the damp, dirty floor. This position once so painful was now a position of rest.

Then various officers came and peered in through the little window, crusted with layers of dirt, into the dimly lighted room, until they saw me squatting with five months' growth of beard that had sprouted in all directions. Each one studied me, then left. Even the prison physician came and looked in at me.

"Evidently the authorities of Ts'ao Lan Tzu," I thought, "have some doubt of my identity. They are not sure if this wildly bearded creature is Rui Ko-Ni or someone else substituting for him."

"But why am I kept in this room? Perhaps they will keep me here until the judge returns from his siesta when he will call me to court and release me. It is now about 1 o'clock in the afternoon."

The door opened and I was ordered out of the room.

"In which direction will I be ordered to go? To the east: to the court room, or to the west: to the cells?"

I was ordered to proceed to the west.

"My," I thought, "I am ordered to a cell, not to the court. This is bad!"

Through the eastern part of this double compound, we passed Section A, and B, where the old cells were in which I had suffered a veritable hell. We entered the western part of the compound. Formerly this was the Chao Yu Pu (Educational Ward) where prisoners who were "progressive" and well advanced in their "reformation" were placed. Here they enjoyed many privileges denied the other prisoners.

Now the Chao Yu Pu had been abolished and the section rebuilt. I was ordered into an empty cell. The door was closed and bolted.

The cell was full of dust. The walls were bare.

"Perhaps I will wait here until two o'clock or later, during the afternoon session of the court, and then be taken to court for my release," I thought, still hoping to be released.

The officer opened the door and gave me a hand broom to clean the cell.

"That is a bad sign. If I am ordered to clean the cell, I must be going to stay here. But perhaps the officer wants me to sweep the kang so I can have a relatively clean place on which to sit."

I swept the kang and then sat on a bundle I had brought in and waited, waited to be called to court.

One, two hours passed. My hopes were low but not gone.

Then the officer opened the door and pasted on the wall a program of the daily order to be observed in the cell. That was the coup de grâce. My hopes of release were killed!

"A daily order," I sighed to myself, "has only one meaning; I am here to stay, how long I do not know, but I am not to be released; on the contrary, I must be here for more punishment. The old hell of Ts'ao Lan Tzu is back!"

That night I did not sleep well. I rolled and tossed on the hard wooden kang, plagued by misgivings of what was in store for me.

·40·

An Encouraging Court Session

"Tso! (Go!)" the Sepo guard said as he stood with his big pistol pointed at me, and motioned me to get going.

It was the afternoon of July 14, 1955. I had been called out of my cell by the officer who handed me over to an armed guard, in traditonal Ts'ao Lan Tzu style.

"I must be going to court," I thought.

"What will happen to me? Am I in for a repetition of the early days at Ts'ao Lan Tzu: days when I was questioned, cajoled, tortured by painful chains, sleepless nights, and the like, pressed to confess 'crimes'?" I said to myself as I walked to the court in anguish.

We stopped in front of Court Room No. 5, next to my former main court room, Court Room No. 4.

The judge ordered us to enter. I passed through the door into the court room and stood at attention before a young judge whom I could not recognize as ever having seen before. My last regular interpreter, a young woman, was there.

"Sit down," the judge said.

"That is an encouraging sign," I thought, as I took my seat.

"How have you been this past year?" the judge asked.

"Since 21 September 1954, when I was sentenced, I have been in a prison factory in the southwest corner of the South City making match boxes. I worked hard, making as many match boxes and as good match boxes as I could, to cut my prison sentence in half," I said, as I struck the air with my right hand, below my suspended left hand as if cutting a hanging sausage with one stroke.

"Yes, the court has received good reports about your labor."

"Well, that is good news!" I thought in great relief.

"What have you been thinking about?" he questioned.

"It was impossible for me to understand the newspapers when they were read or to follow discussions in the study classes, because I do not know Chinese well.

"On June 10, I was moved with many prisoners to an older part of the prison and on June 17, six other foreign prisoners and I were returned to our former building. I had heard that there was danger of war between the U.S.A. and China and I interpreted this return as a preparation to round up all the foreigners, in order to place them in a special prison, as a means of guaranteeing the security of China."

"What would you do if there was a war between China and the U. S. A.?

"Would you join the army as you did in the Second World War?" he continued.

"No," I said. As a matter of fact, I was too old. But I did not tell him that. I had been dropped from the active reserve officers in January 1951, as too old in grade.

"You would not join the U. S. Army. But what would you do?"

This was a loaded question that had to be answered with tact. I thought fast. I thought of a letter my brother Rev. Dr. J. Francis Rigney, had sent me from San Diego, California, which bore a government post office stamp, reading, "Pray for Peace." "So America," I thought, "wants and talks peace, and communist China also says she wants 'peace,' although she undoubtedly and quite arbitrarily attaches a different meaning to the word. But, the term was acceptable to both and I can use it without offending either."

"I would work for peace; I would not want to see my own countrymen killed, neither would I want to see Chinese killed," I said.

"You are not clear. Be clear. What would you do?"

"I would stand for peace. I have seen much of the destruction of the Second World War," I said, as I gave a lengthy description of the destruction I had seen in North Africa from Tunis to Western Egypt; in Italy; in the Rhine Valley, including Cologne, and Aachen; in Normandy; in the London area; in Tokyo. Then I added, "Another world war with atom and hydrogen bombs would be much more destructive."

"Yes, but you are not clear what you would do?"

This kind of conversation went on for some time. Then I thought he might be trying to induce me to join the communist army, as millions of Chinese Nationalist Army prisoners of war had been cajoled or forced into the Red Armies of Mao Tse-tung. I decided to make a clear statement on this point.

"I would not take up arms against my country, the United States of America, or against the armed forces of the U. S. A. Neither would I take up arms against China," I said. As a matter of fact, chaplains are non-combatants, and I was a chaplain in the inactive reserves.

The judge grew angry and shouted back. "No one asks you to take up arms against the American government, in fact you do not have enough courage to do so!"

That was a relief for me. I had made myself clear. I would not be cajoled into fighting my country and the court recognizes this stand and declines to attempt to move me from it.

"If you would be out in society again, would you do any harm towards the 'people'?"

"No," I said.

"I had never harmed the good people of China and would not do so in the future. In the past, I worked to protect them from the evil of Marxist communism and I would continue to do so," I thought to myself.

"What else have you been thinking about?" he said.

"I have been wondering just why I was brought back to Ts'ao Lan Tzu."

"Well, I will tell you," he said after some hesitancy, "You

see you do not know Chinese and consequently cannot follow the indoctrination course. You were brought back here so you could study about the New China in English."

"What a relief," I thought, "he has made a clear statement why I was returned here, not for punishment but for the indoctrination to which I had been exposed, off and on, since my arrest."

"Why did you grow that beard?" the judge asked.

"For two reasons: The first because I thought a beard looked less disorderly than the fuzz that covered my face. We were shaved or sheared in the prison factory every two weeks or half a month. This meant that our faces looked clean one day and unclean or fuzzy 13 or 14 days. The second reason was I wanted to experiment with growing a little beard and mustache. Later I will trim and reduce this present beard."

"If you desire it, I can arrange that you will be shaved daily," he said to my great surprise.

"No, thank you, I am satisfied and want to experiment with growing a beard."

"Very well, you may keep your beard!"

The judge also told me that the court considered me honest, all Catholics honest! This was encouraging indeed.

After a few more questions and answers about trivial matters, the session that had lasted about one and a half hours came to a close.

The judge dismissed me and told me to return to my cell which I did in rather good spirits.

·41·

Solitary Confinement

On July 15, 1955, I was called out and given a thorough physical examination by the prison physician. Among other things he also counted and measured the scars I had on my wrists from handcuffs and on my ankles from fetters, scars I will carry to my grave.

He also made a spinal reflex test by a stroke of a small hammer, below the patella, and then by tickling the skin of the front lower abdomen. The reaction of the kick especially of the right leg was slight, as was the quivering of the skin especially of the right side.

This perplexed me but as the physician spoke no English I was unable to inquire about it from him.

I had been walking with rather stiff lower legs. Cell-mates remarked in the end of 1951, that I walked as though I still had fetters, or like an old woman with bound feet.

I remembered how in August 1951, the judge threatened to cripple me for life, if I failed to confess properly.

"Can it be that I am partly paralyzed or in the early stages of a form of creeping paralysis?" I thought and worried for many days, even to the writing of these memories.

When I told him I had vomited blood in the previous April, he looked much concerned and gave me a chest examination.

He weighed me and found I weighed 101 pounds. I told him I had weighed 180 pounds on being arrested, and that I must have dropped to below 100 before I went to the prison factory where our meals were somewhat better than at Ts'ao Lan Tzu.

On the next day, 16 July, the physician visited me in my cell and told me I was too thin. He inquired about my food and asked me if I liked wo tou. I told him I could eat wo tou but never liked it. He then told me he would order rice for my meals instead of wo tou and advised me to buy one pint of milk a day, to be delivered by the prison kitchen personnel, as well as fresh eggs. I ordered these and received them. From then on, for my last eight weeks in prison, I was given rice which I like very much.

Around the same time, I was really delightfully surprised when a big food package arrived from my family, and a one kilo (or about 2.4 pounds) package from the American Red Cross. Later I received two more such packages from the American Red Cross and even a 5 kilo (11 pounds) box, as well as another big package from my family.

These packages were simply grand, with the instant coffee, cocoa, powdered milk, biscuits, tinned fish and meat, nuts, jellies, etc., they contained.

At first I rationed these supplies eating only two tins a week. The coffee was consumed in as little daily amounts as possible to make the supply last. I had not tasted coffee for four years.

All this was done because I did not know if I would ever receive any more such packages or if I did, whether they might not be suddenly cut off. Often before I was allowed a privilege such as receiving packages from the sisters, then suddenly with no warning they were cut off.

However, when more packages arrived from my family and the American Red Cross sent a 5 kilo package every two weeks, I had to increase my rations, to four tins a week, otherwise my supplies would accumulate and become a double problem. They would be difficult to store in my cell and difficult to transport, if I moved.

I felt very grateful to my family for these splendid packages. Later I learned that a Divine Word Missionary Brother in

Techny, Illinois, had made up some of these packages, send-ing them under my family's name.

I likewise felt very grateful to the American Red Cross for their packages. I thought of the excellent services I had seen the American Red Cross do for the U. S. servicemen in the Second World War. Now they were doing all they could for us civilian prisoners.

The first three or four weeks in Ts'ao Lan Tzu were weeks of hopefulness. Many events pointed to an improvement in my prison status, if not my impending release: the court session, in which the judge said I had worked well and was honest, and had even offered to have me shaved every day; the physical examination; the reception of the food packages; the treatment I received from the officers—these never shouted at me as before.

Each night on retiring, I reviewed and balanced up the events of the day. "This was a favorable indication. That was unfavorable, etc.," I would say to myself. Usually the balance was favorable.

During the period in Ts'ao Lan Tzu, from July 13 to September 11, a little over eight weeks, I was in solitary confinement. This was a great relief, away from all the pushing and pulling; the shouting of chu changs and pen changs; the almost continual forced isolation or persecution from cellmates; the awful tou chenging of myself or other prisoners.

It seemed so restful, to be alone, alone with God.

At times I could hear tou chenging going on in the eastern section. "Shoa! Shoa! Shoa!" from the distance really sounded like the barking of packs of dogs.

When tou chenging was done across the yard from where I was, it sounded louder, more distinct and therefore, not so beastly.

I never felt alone in prison. I was continually mindful of

the Presence of God. Now in solitary, I meditated as I pleased. I made formal daily meditations which had been impossible before. I continued, with more recollection, to pray my three rosaries every day.

I also thought over many problems, as those related to the re-establishment of Fu Jen University.

I thought much about the Gold Coast in West Africa and Achimota College now the University College of the Gold Coast.

St. Mary's Mission Seminary in Techny, Illinois, where I had taught before leaving for the Gold Coast in May, 1939, was often on my mind.

I even thought much about St. Xavier's University in New Orleans, conducted by the Sisters of the Blessed Sacrament.

Around July 17, four days after coming to Ts'ao Lan Tzu, the woman who had served as my interpreter brought me communist literature to read, especially back issues of "The People's China," and "New Times," a weekly publication of Moscow.

She also brought me a book entitled, "Perfidious America." This book was so much anti-American propaganda over the Korean cease-fire. It stated that Americans after the most inhuman cruelties ever perpetrated, had tried every kind of deceit, treachery, etc., to continue the war, to sabotage the cease-fire talks when the "people" of the world had forced them to the peace talks, etc., etc.

A book by a "progressive" was given me to read. I remember how this "progressive" complained so bitterly because he had been hand-cuffed by the police for about half an hour. I thought, "You should have been in communist China and have acted and spoken against the Red government similarly to the way you did against the American government. You would have worn not handcuffs alone but also rusty, dirty, sharp fetters and not for only half an hour but for half a year or more; you would not have been allowed to be free to fly to Nassau for your wedding before being taken out to the Tien Ch'iao to be shot!"

Another book was about the lives of the Rosenbergs. I thought that no one in Red China had had the opportunities of an open trial with their own chosen counsels of defense, as the Rosenbergs had. The communists accused the U. S. A. government of murdering this couple. But they overlooked the hundreds they had murdered in Peking alone, in 1951. On the Easter of that year, 199 were reported in the Red papers as having been executed. In Tientsin, on the same Easter, I was told 250 were executed. I always think of that as "Black Easter."

Another book was a Chinese Red Cross propaganda publication against the Americans, for "forcing" the inhabitants of a certain island to leave before the Reds came. I had never heard of any Red Cross society in the Western World publishing propaganda! I thought of a propaganda booklet about acts of immorality of unnamed U. S. and British servicemen in Korea. This was issued by the Chinese Red Cross Society and I was forced to read it at least six times, in 1953.

Another book was about the so-called Rearmament of Western Germany which I read with great interest, because between the lines I could read that western Europe was reviving to the dismay of the barbarians of the Kremlin.

Around August 20th, my interpreter stopped bringing this literature. This seemed an unfavorable indication. I wondered why this literature was stopped.

Then around September 8, 9, and 10th we had gloomy, rainy days.

On September 10th I was especially depressed. I had been back in Ts'ao Lan Tzu over eight weeks and seemed to be far from being released. My hopefulness of the end of July and early August had died down. It seemed I had entered a new era, but a long one, in prison. So often I had had hopes of being released and just as often these hopes were shattered.

I retired a weary and depressed prisoner that night of the tenth of September, nineteen hundred and fifty-five!

·42·

Released

"TODAY IS SUNDAY, September the eleventh," I said to myself as I scratched off the tenth day of the month on my home-made calendar.

It was a cloudy and chilly day.

After breakfast the assistant head of the prison came to my cell and felt my summer clothing which actually was too light for the chilly days we were then having, and spoke to me in Chinese. I thought he asked me if I had warmer clothing, which I did have and told him so. Then he motioned to put them on and left.

I put on a heavier coat which my family had recently sent me, and thought it was considerate of the officer to show such concern over my comfort.

The same officer soon returned and asked me if I had heavier pants and why I had not put them on. He then motioned me to pack up my belongings.

I was perplexed. I did not know what I was in for.

"Perhaps I am to move to a different cell, perhaps to a different prison reserved for foreigners. There is a slight probability that I be released," I thought. But in the past, my hopes for release had been shattered so often, that I suppressed such hopes this time.

As I was busy packing, another officer came and ordered me to follow him immediately, leaving my unfinished packing.

I followed him, more perplexed.

He ordered me into a jeep.

I was really puzzled.

"Ni shih chu fa yuan," he said. I was not sure whether his words meant, "You are going to the court" or "You are going to another prison."

We drove east, to almost the Tien An Men (Gate of Heavenly Peace) on the Red Square, then turned south to a 3 or 4 storied, yellow building, that looked like a factory.

"My goodness!" I thought. "Another prison factory! Now I will have to start from the beginning at some other trade! It was difficult to learn match box making. Now I will have to start from the bottom at something else."

We stopped in front of this sinister looking building and I was led to a side entrance leading to the basement.

I was led to an empty room with a desk in it.

"This must be the room where new inmates are registered," I thought.

There were bars on the window.

In my depression, I waited for some officer to enter to ask my name, length of sentence, etc.

After about half an hour, no one came. I was puzzled.

Then I asked to go to the toilet.

A guard let me out to the toilet. On the way I passed many empty rooms with their doors opened.

"These do not look like prison cells. Never have I seen so many empty cells in Ts'ao Lan Tzu or Tzu Hsing Lu prisons.

On my return to my room, I looked out through the barred window and noticed that none of the windows on the floors above the basement had bars.

"This is not a prison!" I said to myself in great relief. "This is a court house!"

I was excited.

"I am going to court to have my prison term changed, perhaps shortened or terminated."

I was now hopeful.

In about another half hour, a guard ordered me to follow

him. He led me upstairs to the ground floor. The building seemed quite unoccupied by cadres or people, except for one room to which I was taken.

This room was about 30 feet by 15 feet. About a dozen people, cadres or the like were in it. At the end of the room was a gray haired man, apparently a judge at a desk. To his left were three persons including my ordinary interpreter.

"I am in a court," I thought, excited with hope.

I stood at attention, with my cap in my right hand.

"Ni chiao she ma mind tzu? (What is your name?)"

"Rui Ko Ni (Rigney)," I said without waiting for the interpreter.

"Do you understand what the judge asked you?" the interpreter asked.

"Yes, he asked me my name."

"Where do you live?" the judge continued.

"Li Kwang Ch'iao Nan Chieh I Hao."

Then the judge read a document on his desk. It was short. My hopes reached an all time high.

The interpreter translated the statement of the judge. I was never given the document the judge read or a copy of it. As far as I can remember, it stated that I had worked well in the prison factory, kept the rules of the prison, had recognized my crimes and reformed myself by labor. Therefore my case had been referred to the Supreme Military Court which returned it to the Municipal Court and he ended, "You are released."

I wondered for a moment if I could believe my senses, then spoke.

"Thank you," I said, not wanting to say any more especially in adulation of the communist government.

The judge then motioned me to leave.

It would be difficult to express my feelings.

Four years and two months of hell had come to an end!

Years of prayers had been heard!

Repeated hopes had at long last been realized!

I turned and floated out of the court room, out through the corridor, through the main entrance.

I had entered the building as a prisoner, through the basement.

Now I left through the main entrance as a freed man.

On I floated, down the wide entrance stairs, at the foot of which was a limousine with its doors opened.

I made to get into this but was motioned by the guard to get into the jeep in which I had come.

We drove out of the court grounds.

I was released!

I was free!

Thanks be to God!

·43·

The Journey Out of China Started

On arriving back at Ts'ao Lan Tzu, I was returned to my cell, where I found the door opened: a sign I was no longer a prisoner. I completed packing my belongings and was then taken to an empty room near the drill grounds, where I waited, expecting to be returned to my former residence at Li Kwang Ch'iao Nan Chieh I Hao, the former Fu Jen University.

The judge whom I had seen on July 14th, came with a male interpreter.

He informed me that I had been released because of my good record at the work prison, and because of the policy of leniency of the "People's" government.

"There is one more item about which I would like to inform you," he said.

"There has been a conference at Geneva, Switzerland, on an ambassadorial level of the Ambassadors of the "People's" China and the U. S. government. At this conference an agreement has been reached to exchange civilian citizens of these countries, returning them to their mother country. The British government has agreed to serve as intermediaries of this exchange."

Then I understood one reason at least why I was kept in solitary for eight weeks, prior to my release. The communist government did not want me to learn about these ambassadorial conferences in Geneva from news reports or from cellmates. Apparently they followed this policy of keeping me in the dark so they could the better make their final attempt at

Ts'ao Lan Tzu to brainwash me. Knowledge of these conferences would embolden me, they must have thought, to resist more strongly their indoctrination, their final efforts to turn me against the free world, against my country.

I also understood why I was given a good physical examination in mid July and good food and treatment since July 13th. This was done to build up my poor health, as well as to provide that my last and clearest impressions of the Chinese communists would be good ones.

"What do you plan to do on being released from the prison?" the judge asked.

"I will first go to the dentist for dental care, then I will apply for my exit visa."

"Could you postpone your dental work for two or three days?" he asked.

"Yes, of course I can," I said, as I thought how for about three and a half years I had suffered from toothaches from poor teeth, unable to eat without much pain and had been repeatedly refused my requests for dental care. It would be small matter to wait two or three days.

"The reason for this request is because the 'People's' government will help you leave China as soon as possible."

At noon, tiffin was served me.

"When had I ever seen such a lovely meal served in Ts'ao Lan Tzu?" I thought.

"Scrambled eggs and man tou (white bread, steamed in Chinese style)!" I said to myself as I saw the meal. "I certainly am not a prisoner any longer!"

About 4 o'clock my former ordinary interpreter came and told me to prepare my belongings for a journey.

"Am I going north or south? If I am going south, I will not need the warm clothing that a journey to the north would call for," I said.

After some hesitation she said, "South."

"Southward," I thought, "that means I will leave China

either passing through Shanghai or being taken to the border of Hong Kong."

I prepared a small bundle of light clothing I had for my journey. The rest of my belongings: clothing, bedding, unconsumed tinned food, I prepared and requested be sent to the good Chinese S.Sp.S. sisters (Holy Ghost Missionary Sisters) who had gone to such sacrifice to render me aid whenever they were allowed to. The interpreter said the police would see to it that this request would be carried out.

She then introduced me to two policemen, one of whom she said would take charge of me on my journey out of China. I will call the head of these two guards "Senior" and his assistant "Junior."

About five o'clock, I was driven in a jeep with my two guards to a hotel in the South City. It was clean.

Senior told me I need not leave my room for meals. These would be brought to me in my room. I understood. I was to be confined to my room until departure.

I took a good bath—a bath in a tiled clean bath room, and at my leisure!

What a relief it was to be free to go to the toilet as I wanted to, without being rushed or under the eyes of an armed guard, and with modern, ceramic facilities at my disposal.

A good western meal was served me in western style. I am very fond of Chinese meals and manner of serving them. But I could not but relish to the full this excellent western meal.

I then prayed my Divine Office for the first time in four years and two months. How consoling that was! My old breviary, bearing the ear-marks of a quarter of a century or more of use, worn covers, thumb marks on each page, the back broken, so that the body of pages were split into two separate parts, the ribbons long since worn to shreds.

How dear it was! What memories it recalled! My ordinations as a sub-deacon, deacon, and priest! How beautiful were those psalms, how lovely the various antiphons, how inspiring the lessons! And the Te Deum! that symphony of praise! I prayed it twice that night of September the eleventh nineteen hundred and fifty-five—once for the Divine Office and once as a special prayer of thanksgiving to Almighty God for my release.

That night for the first time in fifty months, I retired when I wanted to and lay on a soft bed with clean white sheets.

For the first time since July 25, 1951, I retired in an unlit room.

How wonderful I felt as I lay on that soft bed, in the dark, telling myself over and over again: "You are free—You are free—You are free!"

I did not sleep much that night, September 11, 1955. How could I!

"How did you sleep last night?" Senior asked me on the morning of September 12, 1955.

"Not very well."

"Yes! I know that. You got up several times, putting on the light of your bedroom. What is the trouble with you? Are you afraid to return to the U. S.?"

"I am not afraid. I have no reason to be afraid to return to my home country. I could not sleep because I was so happy over my release from prison."

In the evening I was told we would leave Peking on a train around 10 o'clock that night.

I asked Senior for my hotel bill. He replied that the "People's" government was paying all my travelling and hotel expenses until I crossed the border of China.

Around 9:30 o'clock that evening we drove to the main railroad station of Peking and shortly afterwards left that beautiful city on the train bound for the south.

·44·

Who Was Brainwashing Whom

THE TRAIN COACHES which were all sleepers were laid out in European style with an aisle to the side opening into compartments. In my car which was first class, each compartment accommodated four passengers. In the second class there were six bunks to a compartment.

In the compartment where I was were my two guards, Senior and Junior, and a fourth man in plain clothes apparently well known to my uniformed police guards. Junior spoke English and was my interpreter and constant companion or guard.

In each compartment were upper and lower bunks on either side. The bunks were open and wooden. A straw mat and a blanket were supplied each passenger for night use.

On Tuesday, September 13, I awoke after a relatively good night's rest, in spite of the hard wooden berth. When I left the compartment to wash and shave, Junior accompanied me. He said he wanted to protect me whenever I left the compartment. He and I took meals in the dining car after the rush was over. The meals were good.

At supper I asked Junior if I were being deported. I concluded I must be undergoing deportation since I could not leave the compartment without one or the other guard accompanying me.

It seemed this question took him by surprise. He hesitated then said, "Do not mistrust the 'People's' government. You are really released and the 'People's' government is helping you to leave China as soon as possible."

As I gathered later, I was not deported technically.

After this question, I was not accompanied by a guard when I went to the toilet or to wash my teeth or face.

Sometime this day, I learned I was to be taken to the border of Hong Kong via Hankow and Canton.

Throughout the journey, from Peking to the Hong Kong border, Junior worked on me. It seemed his efforts were the last attempt of the Chinese communists to indoctrinate me.

I told him in these discussions that I would never become a Marxist because this system is based on dialectical materialism which I could not accept as a Christian and that I did not believe in the communist theory of class warfare and in their practice of confiscating property without compensation of the owner.

I also told him that the communists made a big mistake all over the world by not restricting their theories to economics and politics to the exclusion of religion. I told him that the Church of China would support any government that was not opposed to her religious faith and practices.

He thanked me for these various suggestions and said he would report them to his superiors.

"Are you married, Rigney?" Junior said embarking on a new topic of discussion, after a long silence.

"No."

"Why not?"

"Catholic priests of the Latin rite do not marry."

"Why not? That seems unreasonable to me."

"The celibacy of the Catholic Church had its roots in the example of Christ and St. John the Apostle. Later the PEO-PLE, demanded it. The PEOPLE," I emphasized, "in the early centuries of the western Church preferred a celibate clergy to a married one."

Then after a long period of silence Junior continued, "Rigney, I feel sorry for you. I feel sorry for all Catholic priests because they are not allowed to marry."

"Well, that is what the PEOPLE want," I said, "and the Catholic Church has ever considered, and whenever possible, carried out the will of the PEOPLE!"

When we reached Hankow, Junior and I took breakfast in a little Chinese restaurant. He started his usual discussion about Marxist communism.

"Rigney, you are hopeless. This is clear to me from the discussions we have had so far. You will never be a communist," Junior said.

"Indeed, I will never be a Marxist communist."

"But there is one point on which we agree and that is peace."

"Yes," I replied. "I stand for peace, the peace of Christ."

As our conversation continued I said, "I have profited from our discussions the past two days. An idea has been growing in my mind from these conversations we have had over communism."

"Is that so! What is it?"

"Karl Marx made a big mistake."

"Karl Marx made a mistake?" Junior exclaimed, not a little shocked.

"Yes," I continued, "Karl Marx made a mistake. He elaborated his theory, then worked to make the facts fit the theory. This is unscientific. He should have studied first the facts, evolving his theory on the basis of the facts, making the theory fit the facts, not the facts fit the theory."

Junior did not know much about the writings of Karl Marx, the prophet of the new religion of the worship of the god matter. In fact, I got the impression that the Chinese communists know little about Karl Marx. They are better acquainted with the works of Lenin, the protégé of General Ludendorff, and Stalin, the erstwhile ally of Hitler, and of course the quisling Mao Tse-tung.

Junior did not take me up on this point but shifted the discussion to the question of the existence of God.

"You Christians believe in God. You are not scientific in this."

"Look Junior," I said, "do you see this cup?"

"Yes."

"It is here now, in position A." Then I moved it about a foot and said, "It is no longer in position A, but in a new position, position B."

"Yes."

"The reason the cup passed from position A to position B is not intrinsic, within the cup. The cup does not contain the reason for this change of position. If the cup in position A, contained the reason for being in position B, it would not be in position A but in position B. But it is not in position B but in position A. Therefore, the cup in position A does not contain the reason for being in position B. The reason is external to the cup. In other words the cup must be moved, or as St. Thomas Aquinas put it, 'Everything that moves, is moved by another!' I moved the cup. In turn, I was moved by energy released from the food I recently ate. The food I ate received its energy, was moved by energy from the sun which caused the process of photosynthesis. The sun gets its energy from another source, perhaps the disintegration of atoms and so we proceed from the moved to the external mover until by necessity we must admit the existence of a Being that had the reason for its motion within Itself. That being is God, or Tien Chu or Deus, or Zeus, or Allah, or X or whatever you wish to call It. It is the Unmoved Mover." I explained this proof for the existence of God from other angles.

Soon I began to wonder who was brainwashing whom. Was Junior brainwashing me or was I "brainwashing" Junior?

Farewell China Till We Meet Again

WE ARRIVED in Canton in the afternoon of Thursday, September 15, 1955. Two local policemen joined Senior and Junior as my guards. These four policemen and I drove to a hotel, where I was placed in a room with bath, and told my meals would be brought up to me.

That evening Senior came to my room, with Junior, and read the statement about the agreement reached at Geneva between the U. S. government and the Red government of China to exchange civilian nationals. Junior translated, and I was obliged to give in writing that I had heard and understood this statement.

Senior then took the trouble of getting my Chinese money changed into Hong Kong money. He also purchased half a pound of the best kind of Chinese tea, the Lung Tsing (Green Dragon), because I had said I liked Chinese tea.

He likewise purchased two shirts for me although I had told him I had two shirts and needed no more.

About eleven o'clock as I lay in my bed, planning what to do when I crossed the border of China into Hong Kong, Junior knocked at the door and told me that since I was to spend my last night in China, he would like to sleep in the same room with me, in the second bed that was in the room.

I told him I had no objections.

I thought that the communists feared I might get in touch with someone through the window, or by sneaking out of my room, and therefore had ordered a guard for my room.

On the morning of Friday, September 16, 1955, my four

police guards drove me to the railroad station for my last ride in China.

On this last stretch of my journey, Junior apologized for having argued so much with me over my beliefs.

"You do not like to argue, do you?" he said.

"No, I do not like to argue. If anyone is interested in religion such as Catholicism, I am very willing to explain my religious belief, Catholicism, to him, but I will not argue with him or put pressure on him to accept it."

Then after some time, I explained again to Junior that the "People's" government had no reason to fear the Chinese Catholic clergy. They are willing to labor under any form of government, including the communist government. They only ask the government to grant them religious freedom.

I then wrote a letter to the "People's" government thanking them for what they had done for me, as helping me to leave China, at their expense. I wrote nothing that would deny the inhuman treatment they had dealt me during my imprisonment of four years and two months.

After this Junior told me he and Senior had had a conference and decided to shake hands with me on leaving me at the border.

Junior also said that he hoped I would return to the "People's" China as a friend of the "People."

We were nearing Lo Wu, the station on the China-Hong Kong border.

I had been arrested on July 25, 1951, and released on September 11, 1955. I spent 1509 days in prison. My expulsion journey lasted five days. If these five days be counted, I was 1514 days under police guard in communist China.

Around about noon, we arrived at Lo Wu.

I was placed in an empty room where I waited for about one hour. Senior asked me to write and sign a letter stating that I had travelled from Peking to the border of China without losing anything. This was true so I signed it.

Then the customs officers came and examined my luggage. This being over my guards conducted me out of the station building. I carried a hand bag. They assigned the rest of my baggage to a carrier who carried it for me over the border.

At the southern end of the station, Senior and Junior took leave of me, shaking my hand.

Alone, without police guard, I walked southward, to Her Majesty's Crown Colony of Hong Kong.

I did not know what to expect on arriving in Hong Kong. The communists had helped me to leave China as soon as possible.

"Perhaps," I thought, "the British will expect me to leave Hong Kong as soon as possible. Where will I stay? Will I be welcomed at the Catholic Cathedral? There are no Divine Word Missionaries in Hong Kong to welcome me or to offer me living accommodations while I receive the dental care I need, secure new and proper clothing, etc., and help me obtain transportation to the U. S. A."

I approached the bridge over the Lo Wu river and saw a few uniformed British police. "I will tell them I am Father Harold Rigney and request that they take me to the American consul," I thought.

·46·

Hong Kong: Freedom

"Are you Father Rigney?" one of the Hong Kong police officers said in what an American would improperly call a British accent.

I cannot explain the feelings I experienced when this kind Scotsman spoke to me. His few words were a message of welcome, a message of kindness, such as I had not heard since Lin Piao's Red hordes poured into Peiping on February 1, 1949.

For six years and eight months, with the exception of the last two months when I was accorded better treatment as a last effort to convert me to communistic ideas or sympathies, I had suffered rebuffs, insults, expressions of hatred, persecutions, imprisonment, tortures, false accusations, confiscations, treachery, insecurity, from public authorities in communist China.

Now at last a public authority, a British policeman, spoke kindly, sincerely, friendly, offering me hospitality, me an American, a foreigner.

"Yes, I am Father Rigney," I said and I could have kissed the free soil of Her Majesty's Crown Colony of Hong Kong, which with nearby Portuguese Macao is a haven, a free spot, adjoining the police state of the "People's" China.

The stouthearted Scotsman, A. L. Gordon, Superintendent of Police of Hong Kong, said, "Welcome," and approached me with outstretched hand which I shook, too moved to wring it as I should have.

Then a second British officer, Paul Grace, Superintendent of Police of Hong Kong, approached me and welcomed me, shaking my hand.

"Tsai Chien Chung Kuo (Farewell China till we meet again)," I said to myself and began to cross the bridge over the Lo Wu river, the border of China.

A third British officer, Derrick Pierce, Inspector of Police of Hong Kong, followed suit with a warm welcome.

Father Poletti rushed up to welcome me and give me a letter. This zealous priest, the pastor of Taipo, keeps watch at the border for incoming bishops, priests, brothers and sisters.

Mrs. Margarite Shrathie, Representative of the British Red Cross, came forward to extend a hand of welcome.

Mr. Richard Tomlin, Representative of the American Red Cross came up to welcome me and shake my hand.

Mr. Truman Solvernd, another Representative of the American Red Cross greeted me, shook my hand and welcomed me to freedom.

As long as I live, I shall never be able to express the feelings that overwhelmed me on that occasion. Only one who has gone through the hell of Chinese communist prisons and the brutality of Mao Tse-tung's China would be able to understand my feelings.

I do not remember the questions these kind people asked me or what I replied. I was so excited!

I read the letter Father Poletti gave me and found to my joy that Father Henry Striethorst, S.V.D., whom I had thought was certainly in prison, had escaped arrest and was in Hong Kong.

The police then invited me into the station while a phone call was put through to Father Henry Striethorst, S.V.D., informing him of my arrival.

After this I was given transportation in the beach wagon of the American Red Cross to be driven to Victoria, on Hong Kong Island.

About a thousand feet down the road we met the press and television men. I got off and said to these men, "I have waited four years and two months for this day. I wish to thank Almighty God, the American government, the British government and all who have helped me to realize this day."

I hesitated, then said to the press men and TV men who were there, "I hope none of you will ever have to go through the 're-education' I have gone through."

We then drove on to Kowloon, where we were ferried over to Victoria, and then to the Catholic Center in the King's Building, where I met Father Striethorst, S.V.D.

Father Smith, a Maryknoll Missionary, drove Father Striethorst and me to the S.V.D. Procure at Tung Shan Terrace No. 10, Stubbs Road. On the way we stopped at the American Consulate General where Mr. Robert Aylward, U. S. consul, whom I knew from Peking, came out to greet me.

On arriving at the S.V.D. Procure, I began to learn that all the foreign Divine Word Missionaries were out of China but Father Peter Huengsberg, S.V.D., a prisoner in Ts'ao Lan Tzu, Peking.

I also began to learn that ever so many people had prayed and worked for my release.

I had no doubt that my dear old stepmother, that good soul, a niece of the late Senator George Norris of Nebraska, as well as my brother, sisters and their families, the members of the Divine Word Missionaries and the Holy Ghost Missionary Sisters, prayed unceasingly for my release. But I was surprised and deeply moved to learn that thousands of little children, God bless them, prayed for me and wrote letters of petition on my behalf, as did countless other people in my native and beloved Chicago as well as in other regions as the Gold Coast of West Africa (where much of my heart remains), Ireland, the Philippines and Germany.

I began to understand why the treatment accorded to me in prison started to improve in April 1955.

The effects of my dear, noble sister, Mrs. Mary Anne Hanley, and of that tireless, self-effacing priest: Father Ralph M. Wiltgen, S.V.D., assigned by Divine Word Missionaries in the States to work for my release, began to take effect shortly before this.

Due to their efforts, "The New World" of the Chicago archdiocese, Mr. Thomas Reynolds and "The Chicago Sun-Times," Mr. Joseph B. Meegan and "The Back of the Yards Journal," and N.C.W.C. News Service were informed about my case and began to publicize it and fight for my release in February and March.

As a consequence the Chinese communist government must have decided in April 1955, to prepare to release me.

Senator Paul H. Douglas of Illinois submitted a concurrent resolution (No. 32) on May 5, in the U. S. Senate on my behalf.

Congresswoman Marguerite Stitt Church, Congressmen James C. Murray, John Kluczynski, Charles Boyle, Barrett O'Hara, Melvin Price and John McCormack, spoke on my behalf on the floor of congress.

On October 14, 1955, my sister, Mrs. James (Mary Anne) Hanley, wrote the following:

"I would like to tell you of a man who, I think, is directly responsible for your release. For some time, the family and Fr. Wiltgen had been trying to get different people interested in your case, but we did not have much luck. Then we took it up with Mr. Joseph B. Meegan, who is executive secretary of the Back of the Yards Council. He was unaware of your plight and was amazed at the things we told him regarding yourself. Around the first part of April, Joe Meegan had business in Washington. While there taking care of his business, he called on various members of the State Dept. and they assured him that they were doing all they could for you. When Joe Meegan returned to Chicago, he inaugurated a letter-writing campaign and he publicized it in the Back of the Yards Journal, the Sun-Times and on radio and TV programs. The local representatives got such a deluge of letters that they had to make up form letters in order to answer. I forgot to say that in February 'The New World' published your letter to Jim and me and got a terrific response from the people; people wrote in asking what they could do. Addresses of local representatives were printed; people wrote and that's the way things were until Joe took over. Once Jim was riding on a bus on the North Side of Chicago and he heard some people say on the bus, 'Have you written in for Fr. Rigney yet?'

"Then Joe Meegan decided that we would send all letters directly to President Dwight D. Eisenhower. Fr. Roman J. Berendt, who is president of the Back of the Yards Council, wrote a letter to all priests in the Archdiocese of Chicago. Joe Meegan requested that the sisters and school children of the parochial schools write directly to President Dwight D. Eisenhower. This campaign with the children and sisters and other adults writing to the President, amounted, according to the latest tally, to 65,000 letters which broke a record for any campaign to the White House in the United States. Joe had letters from the principals of over 300 schools telling the numbers of letters their children wrote tallying 65,000. The President answered some of the letters; Ma also received an answer. Through publicity, letters were not only coming from Chicago, but all over the U. S. and foreign countries (Francis and Dorothy started a campaign where they live: San Diego and Muskegon). TV and radio programs were nationally broadcast all over the U. S. Letters came from Canada, the Gold Coast (Africa), Philippines and Germany.

"Later, more letters were written to China in a follow-up campaign; they went to Chou En-lai and Madame Shih Liang. Ma received an answer from Chou En-lai via the Chinese Red Cross; and they invited her over to see you, but our State Dept. vetoed that because of no representation in that country and no assurance of safety.

"On April 23 Fr. Fu, S.V.D., and Fr. Wiltgen made arrange-

ments to celebrate your Silver Jubilee by having a Mass in
your honor, which was open to the public, at St. Augustine's
Church. The Mass was said by Fr. John Fu who was with you
at the University, and a wonderful sermon was given by Fr.
Wiltgen. Many people attended; all the family was there, even
the children. It was a wonderful Mass, tho quite sad because
of your absence. That same day, our Mayor of three days,
Richard J. Daley, who is a good friend of the Council (also
was reared in the Back of the Yards neighborhood), sent a
telegram to the President of the U. S. requesting that he do
everything in his power to secure your release.

"On May 3, Joe and Ma flew to Washington at the Council's expense to confer with the members of the State Dept.,
and this was highly publicized by the newspapers, radio, and
TV all over the U. S., and some newspapers in foreign countries had articles on this. A couple of weeks later, Prime Minister U Nu of Burma was in New York. When Joe found that
out he flew to New York and asked this man if there was anything that he could do in your case. U Nu seemed very interested and after hearing what Joe had to say, he said, 'I think
that this priest should be released.' Joe gave him two memoes
which he took back to Burma late in July.

"Almost every week the Back of the Yards Journal printed
the latest news of your case. Tom Reynolds, the managing
editor of The Chicago Sun-Times, became interested in your
case; and there were almost daily news items in The Chicago
Sun-Times about you, while still encouraging the letter-writing campaign. Our State Dept. had appointed Ambassador
U. Alexis Johnson to meet with Ambassador Wang Ping-nan
of China at Geneva. Tom Reynolds tried to make an appointment with Ambassador Johnson before he left. Joe was willing
to go with Ma to Washington without an appointment. (This
was in the latter part of July.) The two of them, with a woman
reporter from the Sun-Times named Miss Ruth Moore who
was to look after Ma on the trip, were waiting for the plane's

departure at Midway Airport when the reporter was paged to take a phone call. The call from Tom Reynolds advised Miss Moore that he (Reynolds) had arranged an appointment for Joe and Ma with Ambassador Johnson for two days later. Everyone returned home and came back two days later for the trip to Washington, financed by the Chicago Sun-Times. They conferred with Ambassador Johnson; several of our Senators and Representatives were with them. Mr. Johnson assured Joe and Ma that he would not leave the meeting, and would not take care of anything else, until the prisoner situation was taken care of. He said he would place Fr. Rigney's name at the top of the list (he apparently did). Everybody returned home; and during the trip, Miss Moore took good care of Ma.

"After the meetings at Geneva had been going on for about a month, we were told that you were going to be released. About a week later, you arrived in Hong Kong. I never saw anybody so happy in my life as Joe Meegan."

Everywhere in Hong Kong I have received a warm and hearty welcome from the British, American, and Chinese.

Bishop Bianchi and all the local clergy, brothers and sisters welcomed me when they saw me.

Many Chinese refugees, former students of Fu Jen University expressed their welcome, as did Europeans and Americans I knew in Peking.

His Excellency, the Governor, Sir Alexander Grantham honored me with a one-hour interview.

Recently I said a Sunday mass in a parish church. The pastor told the congregation who I was and that I had spent over four years in prison in Peking.

It was a thrill and a consolation to say this parish mass and offer benediction.

After services a Chinese lady asked me to say a mass for her brother. As she spoke to me about him, her eyes became moist then tears began to flow as the heart-stricken woman told me her brother had been arrested some years ago by the Chinese communists. Some time ago her brother wrote, begging the family to send him Hong Kong money to the value of over one thousand U. S. dollars, otherwise he would be killed.

In this way the Chinese communists squeeze money out of people outside China.

This year he wrote and asked his family to write him, giving full details of each member of their family, including a high ranking officer in the Chinese National Army.

The sight of this suffering, weeping Chinese woman, who had been blackmailed out of hard earned money and who was now undergoing an attempted blackmail to force her into spying for the communists, is a memory I shall forever remember, typifying the suffering of the noble, sensitive, patient, courageous, intelligent and industrious Chinese people and the satanic wickedness of the communist government of the misnamed "People's Republic" of China!

·47·

The Harvest

WHAT HAVE I profited from my four years and two months of imprisonment?

Spiritually, educationally, I have made gains.

Physically, I have lost. This is the price for the gains.

Although throughout my imprisonment I was unable to celebrate the Holy Sacrifice of the Mass, to receive Our Blessed Lord in Holy Communion, to visit Our Blessed Lord in the Blessed Sacrament, to pray my Divine Office—all losses of inestimable spiritual value—I did suffer with my Divine Saviour. I also was granted a deeper insight into the bitter sufferings of Our Blessed Lord in His Holy Passion.

Moreover, I am more resolved to save my immortal soul from the eternal Ts'ao Lan Tzu, the unending pains of hell.

Educationally, I profited much. I learned much.

I got a practical insight into applied Chinese communism. Before my arrest, I knew much about communism, especially of the Mao Tse-tung brand, but I learned much more in prison.

I learned that Chinese communists are not to be trusted.

This holds for all of that brood of vipers from Mao Tse-tung who betrayed China to the Kremlin; from the smooth, suave Chou En-lai who has deceived and is still pulling the wool over the eyes of many outstanding statesmen and politicians in many parts of the world, on down to the last received member of the party who is every inch an unthinking puppet, dancing to the hideous tune of his masters, who in turn are controlled by the Kremlin.

I learned something about the nature of the cunning, brutal tactics of world communism that threatens to destroy the age-old and highly cherished liberties of a slumbering, self-satisfied, over-confident free world.

More than ever, I love the Chinese people, the real people, not the tiny, foreign controlled minority that has seized control of China and tyrannizes, brutally tyrannizes the masses of China.

Before my arrest, I felt hurt over the manner in which many of the Fu Jen staff turned on me. During my imprisonment, especially in the early stages, I was often offended over the persecution dealt out to me by many cell-mates.

Now, however, I understand.

Now I realize better than before, what great pressure, inhuman, diabolical, was brought to bear on these poor Chinese who had their families and themselves to consider, who had no powerful government to fight for them as I did.

I have a deeper understanding of chapters IX and XIII, of the Apocalypse, as quoted by Hamish Fraser in his book, "Fatal Star."

"I saw where a star had fallen from heaven to earth. This star was entrusted with the key of that shaft which leads to the abyss. So it opened the shaft which leads to the abyss, and smoke rose from the shaft as smoke rising from the shaft darkened both the sun and the air. And out of the smoke a swarm of locusts spread over the world, endowed with such power for mischief as scorpions have on earth; they were not to injure the grass on the land, the green things that grew there, or the trees; they were to attack men. . . . They had no power to kill, only to inflict pain . . . such pain as a man feels when he has been stung by a scorpion. (When those days come, men will be looking for the means of death, and there will be no finding it; longing to die, and death will always give them the slip). . . .

"And out of the sea, in my vision, a beast came up to land. To it the dragon gave the strength that was his, and great dominion . . . and now the whole world went after the beast in admiration, falling down and praising the dragon for giving the beast all this dominion; praising the beast too. Who is a match for the beast? They asked; who is fit to make war on him? And he was given power of speech, to boast and to blaspheme with, and freedom to work his will . . . so he began to utter blasphemy against God, blasphemy against His Name, against His Dwelling-Place and all those who dwell in heaven. He was allowed, too, to levy war on the saints, and to triumph over them. The dominion given to him extended over all tribes and peoples and languages and races; all the dwellers on earth fell down in adoration of him, except those whose names the lamb has written down in his book of life, the lamb slain in sacrifice ever since the world was made. . . ."

·48·

Epilogue

I HAVE TRIED to tell my experiences of 50 months in the communist prisons of Ts'ao Lan Tzu Hutung (which means the Lane of the Misted Meadows) and Tzu Hsing Lu (which means Reformation Street) of Peking, the capital of the "Chinese People's Republic," a communist state.

Such is a very difficult task in memoirs of this size.

I have tried to be objective. I have recounted acts, of course, false confessions for which I am ashamed although they were made under duress and delusion. Moreover, I later corrected them by denying them, under threat of execution.

In spite of tortures and cajolery, I did not make the confessions and stick to them, that the communists wanted.

For three years they tried to induce me to confess being an agent of the U. S. government, and that the American Divine Word Missionary organization was under the control of the U. S. government. These appeared to me to be their main objectives. But I remained firm, refusing to admit these outrageous and ridiculous charges. As a consequence, I received a long prison sentence.

Often I expected and was ready to be shot. On one occasion I walked to what I thought was my execution grounds and I did not waver. I was prepared to die.

On another occasion, I thought my cruel judge and his aides would tear me to pieces, dismember me.

All these violent tortures only made me more stubborn. I was prepared that night to die, to be literally torn to pieces.

Yet later, under an accumulation of prolonged, relatively light tortures when my conscious mental faculties were seemingly functionless, I confessed falsely. But on coming to myself again, I denied these false confessions.

Had I been shot or torn to pieces, I would have been remembered as a martyr. But the cunning, diabolical, Chinese communists do not want to make martyrs. They prefer to reduce their victims to a sub-human, non-human, non-volitional stage, so they easily confess, truthfully or falsely.

The compromised prisoners lead lives of disgrace—reproaching themselves and, if released, perhaps reproached by others.

They are mentally, physically crippled.

The Chinese communists make disgraced mental cripples, not martyrs.

After arriving in Hong Kong, I related some of my prison sufferings to a Russian, who lived in Russia until 1923, when he left. He had seen much of the cruelty of the Russian Bolsheviki communists. He said, "The Chinese communists employ a subtilty in their tortures, unknown even to the Russian communists.

"The Russians lined up prisoners and shot them, sometimes mowing down masses of them with machine guns, but the Chinese communists do worse, they use subtile, refined, cunning tortures of which the Russians are ignorant and which are worse than death."

Although martyrdom has been denied me, I beg my readers not to be ashamed of my witness for the Lord, but to enter into the spirit of my sufferings for the gospel and to willingly give witness yourselves.

In the words of Blessed Paul, I might say:

"I preach the gospel, and in its service I suffer hardship like a criminal, yes, even imprisonment. . . . What persecutions I underwent! And yet the Lord brought me through them all safely." (2 Timothy 2:8-9, 3:11)

The Divine Word Mission
10 Tung Shan Terrace,
Stubbs Road,
Hong Kong

21 December, 1955
The Feast of the Holy
Apostle: Saint Thomas